BIGGER, BETTER FUNDED AND FOCUSED ON PUBLIC GOODS

How to revamp the European Union budget

Zsolt Darvas, Roel Dom, Marie-Sophie Lappe,
Pascal Saint-Amans and Armin Steinbach

BRUEGEL BLUEPRINT SERIES

Bigger, better funded and focused on public goods: how to revamp the European Union budget

Zsolt Darvas, Roel Dom, Marie-Sophie Lappe, Pascal Saint-Amans and Armin Steinbach

Editor: Stephen Gardner

Layout and cover design: Hèctor Badenes Rodríguez

Bruegel

33, rue de la Charité, Box 4

1210 Brussels, Belgium

www.bruegel.org

ISBN: 978-9-078910-64-0

Acknowledgements

The authors are particularly grateful to Jeromin Zettelmeyer for his extensive comments on preliminary drafts. They also thank Marco Buti, Aurélie Catallo, Marek Dabrowski, Hans Geeroms, Heather Grabbe, Francesco Papadia, Lucio Pench, Jean Pisani-Ferry, Elsa Regnier, André Sapir, Simone Tagliapietra, Nina Vujanovic and Guntram Wolff for insightful discussions, comments and suggestions. Participants at the Bruegel workshops on 19 February 2025 and 23 June 2025 and at a discussion with Bruegel members on 23 May 2025 provided valuable feedback and perspectives. Special thanks go to Stephen Gardner for his outstanding editorial work, as well as to Hèctor Badenes Rodríguez for the superb layout of this blueprint.

This publication is based on research funded in part by the Gates Foundation. The findings and conclusions contained within are those of the authors and do not necessarily reflect positions or policies of the Gates Foundation.

Contents

About the authors

Zsolt Darvas is a Senior Fellow at Bruegel and at Corvinus University of Budapest. Before joining Bruegel in 2008, he worked for the Central Bank of Hungary and the Argenta Financial Research Group in Budapest. His research interests span macroeconomics, international economics, finance, European Union governance and social policy. His current work focuses on policy-related issues, including European economic governance, the EU budget, EU enlargement, income and wealth inequality, and fiscal and monetary policies.

Roel Dom is a Research Fellow at Bruegel and a visiting professor at the University of Antwerp. His research focuses on public finance, taxation and international development. Before joining Bruegel, Roel held various policy and research positions, including as a policy advisor to Belgium's Deputy Prime Minister and an economist at the World Bank. He has a PhD in economics from the University of Nottingham and degrees from the London School of Economics and the University of Antwerp.

Marie-Sophie Lappe is a Research Assistant at Bruegel. She has a master's degree in economics and finance from the University of Tübingen. Her studies focused on quantitative macroeconomics and finance. Previously, she worked in the European Central Bank's International Policy Analysis Division, where she monitored developments in commodity, bond and equity markets.

Pascal Saint-Amans is a Non-resident Fellow at Bruegel. He was Director of the Organisation for Economic Co-operation and Development Centre for Tax Policy and Administration, where he led the international tax reform until 2022. Previously, he served in different tax policy positions in the French finance ministry. From 2000 to 2004, he was financial director of the French energy regulation agency. A graduate of Sciences-Po and École Nationale d'Administration, he is an associate professor at HEC Paris and founding chairman of Saint-Amans Global Advisory.

Armin Steinbach is a Non-resident Fellow at Bruegel, Jean Monnet Professor of Law and Economics at HEC Paris and Research Affiliate at the Max Planck Institute for Research on Collective Goods in Bonn. Previously, he held academic posts at Oxford University, the European University Institute in Florence, the University of St. Gallen and Harvard University. He was a civil servant in the German finance and economy ministries.

Foreword

Bruegel Blueprints are multichapter studies that analyse a policy topic in depth. They normally collect contributions by many authors with different viewpoints. In rare cases, we use the format to provide a consistent vision – literally, a blueprint – written by one team of authors, on how a particular policy design problem could be solved.

The present Blueprint on the reform of the European Union's budget fits in the second category. Its purpose is to inform and influence the debate on the EU's next, 2028-2034 multiannual financial framework (MFF). Drawing on a set of preceding Bruegel studies on the economic and legal foundations of the EU budget, it analyses the composition, financing, and expenditure control mechanisms of the European budget and makes suggestions on how to improve them. It also discusses the consequences of EU enlargement on the MFF.

The importance of the topic can hardly be overstated. As emphasised by the Draghi (2024) and Letta (2024) reports and Bruegel's 2024 Memos to the European Union Leadership, achieving the main public policy goals of the EU – higher productivity growth, greening the economy, safeguarding its security, all while maintaining social cohesion – requires better policy coordination and delegation at the EU level. The EU budget is the single most important instrument for structuring and funding such collective action. While this is true for any EU budget, the challenges faced by the next one are particularly daunting. Most EU governments face tight borrowing constraints and are trying to reduce their deficits. Virtually all EU governments face pressures to spend more on defence and public investment. This makes the efficiency of spending and revenue collection even more important than in preceding budgetary periods.

The essential message of the Blueprint is that maximising this efficiency requires a transformation of the EU budget in at least four respects.

First, a change in the composition of the EU budget towards EU public goods, away from spending that could also be efficiently provided at the national level.

Second, a larger budget, capable of funding and structuring public investments and of spending that benefits the EU as a whole: on innovation, the green and digital transition, cross-border infrastructure, EU partnerships and foreign economic policy (including international climate action).

Third, a shift in the composition of revenue away from member state contributions based on national income towards revenues that are linked to common EU competencies or policy objectives, in areas such as trade, climate and defence. This may or may not increase the fiscal resources available for the EU as a whole. But it would give beneficial incentives to member states and improve the quality of spending by weakening the link between what member states provide and what they expect to receive back from the EU.

Fourth, a strengthening of the framework ensuring the quality of EU spending intermediated by national or local authorities, drawing on the experience of the Recovery and Resilience Facility. Importantly, this means addressing the shortcomings in the performance framework governing that facility, rather than transposing them to the MFF.

Another important conclusion of this Blueprint is that the financial burden of prospective enlargement on the EU budget would be manageable, and that the national economic and fiscal benefits of enlargement could partially, or even fully, offset the associated budgetary costs.

We hope that our Blueprint will support and reinforce the efforts of the European Commission, European Parliament and EU members in shaping the next medium-term budget to address the EU's most urgent challenges and to advance its long-term transformation.

Jeromin Zettelmeyer, Director of Bruegel
July 2025

1 Introduction

The European Union faces growing pressure to deliver on priorities that are increasingly European in nature. Challenges including the climate and digital transitions, competitiveness, economic resilience, defence, migration management and foreign policy go beyond national borders and demand coordinated and well-resourced responses. But the EU's main financial instrument, its budget – or Multiannual Financial Framework (MFF) – remains stuck in the past, with only limited changes from one cycle to the next. Pressures including the COVID-19 pandemic, Russia's war against Ukraine, soaring energy prices and rising geopolitical and economic fragmentation, have increasingly exposed the limitations of the current EU budget system.

This Blueprint sets out how the MFF can be reformed to better match the EU's objectives. It deals with four main issues: the composition and size of EU spending, the revenue system (known in EU jargon as 'own resources'), design of a more performance-oriented budgetary method and the fiscal implications of possible EU enlargements.

Chapter 2 examines how EU spending should be refocused to deliver European public goods (EPGs), or goods that would be more effectively provided collectively at the EU level than by national governments. It introduces a methodology to classify EU spending according to its alignment with EPG principles, dividing current MFF spending into four categories: EPGs, national public goods, EU policy preferences or integrationist objectives, and non-public goods. A main message is that the MFF should focus on EPGs and some integrationist objectives, while other expenditures should be shifted to national budgets. This would free resources for new priorities including climate action, cross-border connectivity, defence and competitiveness.

Chapter 2 also presents a granular analysis of the EU's desirable contribution to additional spending needs. While it draws on earlier estimates of spending gaps, it goes beyond such estimates by distinguishing between public and private spending requirements and, within public needs, the desirable share allocated to the EU budget versus national budgets. The guiding principle of the analysis is the concept of EPGs. The chapter also highlights trade-offs between shifting non-EPG spending to national budgets and increasing the MFF's overall size. The results point to the need for a substantial EU budget increase, even with maximum reallocation.

Chapter 3 turns to the revenue side of the EU budget. It clarifies that since the EU lacks tax-raising powers and nearly all its revenue originates from national budgets, introducing new revenue-raising mechanisms (new 'own resources') or increasing contributions based on the gross national incomes of member countries is immaterial for the total amount raised, but affects how much each country contributes. Nevertheless, there are good reasons for introducing new revenue mechanisms, because they may help to achieve EU policy objectives and might help counter the net-balance calculations that dominate budget debates.

Chapter 3 also reviews current revenue sources, and those proposed by the European Commission, European Parliament and academia, and introduces a new proposal: a defence spending shortfall levy. This would encourage more equitable contributions to European security by countries that currently underspend on defence. The chapter also highlights persistent anomalies in the rebate system that distort the fairness of EU budget contributions.

Chapter 4 analyses how to improve the effectiveness of EU spending by reforming the budgetary method. It endorses the ideas, put forward by the European Commission in February 2025, of applying a performance framework to funds managed by EU countries and of centralising competitiveness and foreign policy instruments. However, it finds that current frameworks, especially in the Recovery and Resilience Facility (RRF), cohesion policy and the Common Agricultural

Policy (CAP), fall short of genuine performance-based budgeting. The chapter also critiques the flawed mainstreaming of horizontal priorities, such as climate action, which overstates the climate impacts of EU spending. It draws out lessons on how to strengthen performance frameworks and design better methodologies for tracking horizontal priorities.

Chapter 5 evaluates the fiscal impacts of possible EU enlargements. It argues that the impact assessment related to any addition of new EU members should cover both the EU budget and national budgets. Russia's war against Ukraine, which has reshaped the geopolitical landscape of Europe, has opened the EU's doors to up to nine new members. The low level of economic development in all of these nine candidate countries, and Ukraine's huge agricultural sector, could have profound implications for the EU's current two largest spending programmes: cohesion policy and the CAP. These pressures have sparked concerns that the financial burden of enlargement could strain the EU's finances.

While there are significant uncertainties in estimating the fiscal consequences of enlargement, particularly related to the timing of accessions, transitional arrangements and potential revisions of allocation rules, chapter 5 concludes that the fears of an excessive financial burden are exaggerated and the financial impact of enlargement on the MFF would be manageable. Moreover, the chapter highlights that the assessment of the overall financial impact of enlargement should also take into account the economic and fiscal gains that enlargement would generate for current EU members and their national budget revenues.

Together, these chapters offer a comprehensive, evidence-based reflection on how the EU budget system must evolve to support a more capable and effective Union. The analysis has important implications for policy. The final chapter summarises the recommendations.

2 Refocusing EU budget expenditures on European public goods

2.1 Context

The European Union faces significant pressure to spend in areas that would benefit the EU as a whole, related to its green transition, competitiveness or foreign economic policy. Yet a substantial portion of its current spending does not contribute directly to such European public goods (EPGs). Evaluating how EU financial resources can be allocated more effectively to ensure that spending aligns with EU-level priorities is hence crucial[1].

The EU's Multiannual Financial Framework (MFF) is central to the provision of EPGs, as it structures EU spending over a seven-year period and determines the financial resources for various policy areas (Buti *et al*, 2024). In this context, this chapter first assesses which current MFF expenditure categories do not align with the EPG objective, thus offering scope for restructuring and reallocation away from non-EPGs to serve European priorities better.

Second, this chapter quantifies the EU's desirable contribution to additional spending needs, distinguishing between public and private spending. Within public spending, it examines the optimum share that should be allocated to the EU budget relative to national budgets. Various studies have been published on the overall investment gap the EU faces – an important component of additional spending needs.

1 IMF (2024) made similar recommendations.

Some research also covers EPGs that do not constitute investment. But these studies often take an agnostic view - or fail to disclose their assumptions - on the division between public and private spending, or the split between EU and national public financing. Some assume that historical spending patterns will continue to apply. Instead of relying on this assumption, our analysis evaluates various components (through the lens of the EPG concept) to determine the optimal share of public spending and, within that, the appropriate allocation between the EU and national budgets.

Third, this chapter assesses trade-offs between reallocation of current non-EPG spending and the desirable increase in the overall MFF. Reallocation of the maximum possible amounts from non-EPG spending to EU-level spending priorities would reduce the required increase in the EU budget. However, the political economy of reducing non-EPG expenditures in the EU budget is likely to raise challenges. In that case, an even larger MFF may be required, if EU-level spending priorities are to be met.

Currently, there are more than a dozen EU facilities outside the MFF (see annex 2 for a list). Various factors have justified the establishment of these off-budget instruments. For example, the EU Treaties prohibit the purchase of military equipment, which is why military support for Ukraine and other partners is provided through the European Peace Facility[2]. Within the MFF, earmarking of specific revenues for particular expenditures is in principle not permitted. However, EU countries agreed to allocate part of revenues from the EU Emissions Trading System (ETS) to the EU level on the condition that these funds are used for climate-related objectives, leading to the creation of the Innovation Fund, the Modernisation Fund and the Social Climate Fund, which are outside the MFF. NextGenerationEU (NGEU), the EU's pandemic recovery and structural transformation instrument, is another major

2 See Council of the EU, 'European Peace Facility', https://www.consilium.europa.eu/en/policies/european-peace-facility/.

facility outside the MFF. It enabled large-scale, temporary and debt-financed EU-level support in response to the COVID-19 crisis. Including it within the MFF framework might have led fiscally conservative EU countries to worry that such temporary spending could become permanent. Incorporating it into the MFF would also have complicated its financing via common EU borrowing.

The list of off-budget facilities could be extended by a new instrument to support common defence projects[3], possibly based on an intergovernmental agreement that also involves non-EU countries such as the United Kingdom and Norway. Peace, a crucial EPG, is ensured through defence and military spending, but the EU does not have and is unlikely to develop a common army. Defence remains the responsibility of individual EU countries, which maintain their armies while coordinating their defence and military operations through EU and NATO mechanisms. Common funding mechanisms for defence need to be outside the MFF for legal reasons (the EU Treaty prevents military expenditure from being included within the MFF) and because such mechanisms arguably should include European democracies that are not EU members (Wolff *et al*, 2025; Zettelmeyer *et al*, 2025).

Another critical issue is the EU's ability to respond effectively to crises. The EU has financing facilities in place to address sovereign debt crises (European Stability Mechanism, Balance of Payments Facility, Macro-Financial Assistance) and banking crises (Single Resolution Fund). However, the EU lacks instruments to respond effectively to emergencies that require significant EU-wide spending, such as the COVID-19 pandemic or the 2015-2016 migration crisis. A dedicated emergency fund that can be mobilised swiftly would provide the flexibility to address unexpected challenges without diverting resources from EPGs within the MFF. Swift mobilisation could be ensured by defining in the regulation governing the fund the types of emergency

3 See for example, Economic and Financial Affairs Council, 13 May 2025, 'Main results,' https://www.consilium.europa.eu/en/meetings/ecofin/2025/05/13/.

the fund could address and the decision-making process to access the fund – for example, qualified majority voting of EU countries based on a European Commission proposal.

Whether this fund is placed inside or outside the MFF is a secondary concern. However, positioning it outside the MFF may help reassure fiscally conservative EU countries that these funds will not be redirected toward unrelated expenditures. Moreover, borrowing seems to be an ideal source of financing for an emergency instrument, similarly to NGEU, and it might be easier for EU countries to agree if the fund is outside the MFF.

2.2 European public goods as a benchmark for the MFF

2.2.1 Definition of European and national public goods

Traditional economic thinking defines public goods as being characterised by non-rivalry (ie the consumption of the good by someone does not diminish the consumption of others) and non-excludability (ie the good can be consumed by anyone) (Samuelson, 1954). Because markets cannot provide these goods in sufficient amounts, a collective-action dilemma arises due to free riding on the efforts of others in providing these goods. This necessitates the involvement of the state, either through the alteration of incentives to stimulate sufficient market supply, or through direct provision of the public good in question.

Public goods can be natural (such as clean air) or human-made (such as public health or defence). One can further distinguish between public goods (ie non-rival and non-exclusive in consumption), such as environmental protection or the internal market (Coutts, 2017); common resource goods (non-exclusive but rival in consumption) such as water resources, the use of infrastructure or central bank liquidity (Berith, 2017); and club goods (exclusive but non-rival) such as the euro area or the Schengen area (Fuest and Pisani-Ferry, 2019). For our purposes, all such goods will be referred to as public goods (Buti *et al*, 2023).

In the European multilevel governance context, a pivotal issue is determining whether a particular public good should be provided at national or European level. Fiscal federalism develops the normative case for assigning responsibilities to different tiers of government and for shaping the interactions between levels of government (Oates, 1972; Begg, 2009). The theory sets out three benchmarks that determine the governance level at which public goods should be provided: externalities, economies of scale and preference homogeneity (Tiebout, 1956).

Based on these, the theory suggests that decentralised provision is the optimal solution when it costs less to provide public goods at a lower rather than higher level, and when there are no benefits in terms of economies of scale by providing the good at the central level. Another argument for decentralised provision arises when there is no benefit from avoiding a negative externality (or creating a positive externality), in case the actions of one country impact negatively on the provision of a public good in another country. On the contrary, centralised provision is advisable if it reduces negative externalities, creates gains in economies of scale and reduces costs. Lastly, similar preferences can be a basis for central provision of a public good if the costs associated with a uniform good are less than the costs of tailor-made national public goods.

A European public good may thus be defined as a good that is undersupplied without public intervention, and which should be provided at EU level to internalise externalities and reap benefits of scale, while ensuring that local preferences are taken into account. In other words, the optimal level of provision of a public good is that which reaps efficiency gains, while taking into account local preferences (Claeys and Steinbach, 2024).

2.2.2 Classification of EU budget spending

In this chapter, we classify EU budget spending into five categories:

- European public goods (EPGs),
- National public goods (NPGs),
- EU policy preferences or integration objectives,
- Non-public goods,
- Unspecified other spending.

The governance of public goods involves rule-setting, financing and delivery. At one end of the spectrum are full EPGs, such as pan-European research initiatives (eg Horizon Europe), cross-border infrastructure projects (eg the Connecting Europe Facility) and international EU activities, including foreign policy, development assistance and climate finance. These goods are characterised by EU-level rule-setting, financing and delivery. At the other end of the spectrum are full NPGs, such as cultural policy, for which rule-setting, financing and delivery is done at national level. Table 1 provides a framework for distinguishing different governance structures for public goods in the EU. The variable combinations of rule-setting, financing and delivery reflect the hybrid nature of many public goods, notably where trade-offs exist between economies of scale, cross-border externalities and differences in national preferences.

Between full EPGs and NPGs, several intermediate cases exist, for which responsibility is shared in different ways:

- Member-state-delivered EPGs: public goods for which rule-setting is done at EU level and financing comes from the EU budget, but delivery is handled by national governments. Examples include crisis-response mechanisms such as NextGenerationEU (NGEU).
- Member state-funded EPGs: in these cases, rules are set at EU level and delivery is managed by the EU, but financing comes from national contributions. Examples include macro-financial stability

mechanisms such as the European Stability Mechanism (ESM) and security initiatives such as the European Peace Facility.

- Coordination public goods: areas in which the EU sets rules but does not finance or directly deliver services. Instead, national governments implement policies in line with EU coordination mechanisms. Examples include state aid rules, the EU fiscal framework and national industrial strategies shaped by EU frameworks.
- EU-funded integration objectives or NPGs: these cases involve EU financing for initiatives that are primarily national in scope but align with broader EU integration goals. Examples include regional cohesion funding (eg EU cohesion and regional funds) and health initiatives such as some aspects of EU4Health.
- Member state-funded EPGs: in some areas, rule setting is national, but EU-level institutions manage the delivery and financing is provided by member states. Examples include joint vaccine procurement programmes and coordinated defence procurement (for instance, through the European Defence Agency, EDA).
- Member state-provided EPGs: many goods that meet our EPG definition – publicly provided, involve strong EU-wide externalities and should be provided at EU level – are currently designed, financed and delivered at national level for historical reasons, or because the financing is not available at EU level. This includes most defence spending and significant spending on partnerships and development that benefit the EU as a whole.

Understanding the distinction between these categories is essential in order to evaluate the efficiency and appropriateness of EU budget allocations. While full EPGs justify EU-level funding and delivery, spending on NPGs or integration objectives requires careful scrutiny to ensure alignment with European priorities. Identifying areas in which reallocation of resources can better support EPGs will be a key consideration in discussions on the future of the MFF.

Furthermore, while military and defence policies remain primarily a national responsibility because of EU Treaty provisions, hybrid approaches such as the European Peace Facility or joint procurement through the EDA illustrate how some aspects of security policy can be coordinated at the EU level without falling under the MFF. Similarly, emergency response mechanisms - whether inside or outside the MFF - must be designed to ensure swift action.

Table 1: The current governance of public goods in the EU

Rule-setting	Financing	Delivery	Examples
EU	EU	EU	Full EPG: Research (Horizon Europe), infrastructure (Connecting Europe Facility)
EU	EU	National	Nationally-delivered PG: Crisis resolution (NGEU)
EU	National	EU	Nationally -funded PG: Macro stability (ESM), security (European Peace Facility)
EU	National	National	Coordination PG: National Industrial and economic policies (state aid, fiscal rules)
National	EU	National	EU-funded integration objectives or PG: Regional cohesion (EU Cohesion Funds, Regional Funds), Health (EU4Health)
National	National	EU	Nationally -funded PG: Security (procurement coordination)
National	National	National	Nationally -provided PG: Most defence, MS-level development assistance
National	National	National	Full NPG: Eg Cultural policy

Source: Bruegel. Note: the table shows the current governance of public goods (PGs) in the EU. In some cases of path dependency, PGs should be provided under different governance types (eg defence).

By analysing the governance structure of EU-funded initiatives through the lens of EPGs and NPGs, we can better assess the scope for reallocation within the EU budget and the optimal balance between national and EU-level responsibilities.

2.3 Assessing MFF expenditures through the lens of European public goods

The 2021-2027 MFF structures EU expenditures under seven headings, further broken down into subheadings and spending lines. Here, we evaluate the extent to which EU budget allocations under each 2021-2027 MFF heading contribute to the provision of EPGs, by assessing each major programme or policy area against the criteria discussed in section 2.2:

- Public or private character: is the good non-rival and non-excludable across EU countries?
- Scale and scope efficiencies: can centralised EU provision cut costs or improve effectiveness compared to national provision? Does EU involvement bring added value?
- Presence of externalities: does provision or under-provision in one country affect others? Are there weakest-link or aggregate-effort dynamics?
- Preference similarity: do EU members have similar interests in how the good is provided?
- EU treaty obligations and integration objectives: are programmes motivated primarily by legal or political commitments (eg redistribution), without meeting EPG criteria?

This framework allows us to go beyond formal EU classification and assess the economic rationale for EU-level provision. Where only some components of a programme can be considered EPGs, we apportion spending accordingly, based on content and regulatory objectives. In ambiguous cases, legal definitions and programme objectives (as set out in EU regulations) were used to guide classification. Detailed assessments by heading can be found in annex 1.

2.3.1 Overview of the MFF's seven main headings and their EPG relevance

Based on detailed assessments (annex 1), our main findings for the seven headings can be summarised as follows (amounts in brackets show the total allocation to each heading in the 2021-2027 MFF; see also Figure 1):

Heading 1: Single market, innovation and digital (€150 billion)

This heading includes programmes that support research and innovation (eg Horizon Europe), digital transformation and the development of cross-border infrastructure through the Connecting Europe Facility (CEF). Horizon Europe and Euratom clearly qualify as EPGs, given their support for knowledge creation and coordination across borders. CEF projects (energy, transport, digital) also offer cross-border spillovers. However, parts of the Digital Europe Programme and InvestEU focus on private goods or national interests, such as support for small and medium-sized enterprises (SMEs), artificial intelligence (AI) development and regional hubs. The space programmes Galileo and Copernicus generate shared benefits and economies of scale and are thus also classified as EPGs. Overall, this heading contains a substantial share of EPG-aligned spending, especially in cross-border research and infrastructure.

Heading 2: Cohesion, resilience and values (€427 billion)

As the largest MFF heading, Heading 2 primarily funds regional and social redistribution through the European Regional Development Fund (ERDF) and the European Social Fund Plus (ESF+). These instruments target economic convergence, labour market integration and social inclusion, which are legitimate EU policy goals, but not public goods in the strict economic sense. Redistribution is driven by political commitments rather than cross-border efficiency gains. Exceptions include some ERDF-funded infrastructure projects and the Cohesion Fund, which support climate action and cross-border transport, which are clear EPGs.

Programmes such as Erasmus+ do support mobility and integration across borders and are considered EPGs. Nonetheless, less than half of this heading contributes to EPGs; the rest is better characterised as integration-oriented redistribution.

Heading 3: Natural resources and environment (€400 billion)

This heading is dominated by the Common Agricultural Policy (CAP), which supports income for farmers and rural development through the European Agricultural Guarantee Fund (EAGF) and European Agricultural Fund for Rural Development (EAFRD). While food security has some public-good aspects, the CAP relies heavily on direct income support and sectoral subsidies, which are not conducive to food security but are rather policy preferences. Environmental objectives (eg eco-schemes) and programmes such as the Programme for Environment and Climate Action (LIFE) do align with EPG principles by targeting global challenges such as biodiversity and climate change. The Maritime and Fisheries Fund addresses negative externalities such as overfishing, qualifying as an EPG. However, these EPG components represent a minority of the total. The CAP continues to reflect national-sectoral support rather than EU-wide public goods provision.

Heading 4: Migration and border management (€26 billion)

Migration and border security involve cross-border interdependence and weakest-link dynamics, especially within the Schengen Area. Asylum systems and external border management in one country affect all EU members. Programmes such as the Asylum, Migration and Integration Fund (AMIF) and the Integrated Border Management Fund address these issues and support the Common European Asylum System. Funding here helps mitigate spillovers from poorly coordinated migration responses and strengthens the EU's collective external border. Since the effectiveness of border control depends on all members, these programmes are strongly aligned with the definition of EPGs. Almost all of Heading 4 spending can thus be classified as EPG expenditure.

Heading 5: Security and defence (€14 billion)

Spending under this heading supports internal security and safety of European citizens, strengthens Europe's defence capacities and provides the tools needed to respond to internal and external security challenges, which EU countries alone are not able to deal with effectively. Security challenges are highly interdependent: terrorism, organised crime and other threats cross national borders and require coordinated responses. The Internal Security Fund and nuclear decommissioning programmes are classic EPGs, preventing negative spillovers and benefitting all EU countries. The European Defence Fund and Military Mobility initiative are intended to tackle defence market fragmentation and enable cost-efficient, interoperable EU military capabilities. Defence policy is increasingly recognised as an area in which EU-level economies of scale and positive externalities are significant, even if direct military expenditures cannot be financed by the MFF because of limitations laid down in the EU treaty. As such, this heading represents a nearly full allocation to EPGs.

Heading 6: Neighbourhood and the world (€110 billion)

External relations, development assistance and neighbourhood policy account for a substantial share of this heading. Many of the funded activities, such as climate action, conflict prevention and sustainable development, are global public goods. Programmes such as the Neighbourhood, Development and International Cooperation Instrument (NDICI), humanitarian aid and pre-accession assistance advance EU values and help stabilise neighbouring regions. While some components (eg humanitarian aid or the Common Foreign and Security Policy) include national preference elements, the rationale for EU-level coordination is strong. Shared objectives, institutional scale and the need for a unified external voice support their classification as EPGs. As a result, Heading 6 is fully EPG-aligned, though national competences still coexist.

Heading 7: European public administration (€83 billion)

Spending under this heading funds the institutions of the EU, including the European Commission, the European Parliament, the EU Court of Justice and related services. These institutions support the legal, regulatory and governance framework underpinning the single market and other EU-level activities. Their services are non-rival, non-excludable and produce EU-wide benefits, including legal certainty and harmonised application of rules. The cost-efficiency of a single supranational administration versus 27 replicated national efforts also supports the classification of administration as an EPG. Despite political debates about administrative efficiency, all spending under Heading 7 is considered EPG spending based on both function and institutional necessity.

2.3.2 Summary of our findings

All current MFF budget headings involve at least some spending on EPGs. For the smaller headings (in monetary terms), most spending can be considered as spending on EPGs, but parts of the two largest headings – cohesion policy and the CAP – fall into the category of integration objectives (cohesion policy) and policy preferences (direct income transfers under the CAP).

For spending under the next MFF to be fully aligned with EPG criteria, around half would have to be re-allocated (Figure 2). Re-allocation could take different forms: spending on NPGs or policy preferences could be nationalised, while spending on integration policies cannot be funded at national level because of their re-distributive nature at EU level. We thus do not propose an elimination of EU spending on integration policies from the next MFF. Consequently, the potential for reallocation of MFF spending from non-EPGs to EPGs amounts to about 0.3 percent of EU GNI. This would include reallocation to EPGs of resources currently spent on NPGs, policy preferences and non-public goods. In the rest of this chapter, we explore whether such a reallocation can plug the EU investment gap.

Figure 1: Headings 1-7 by categorisation of spending

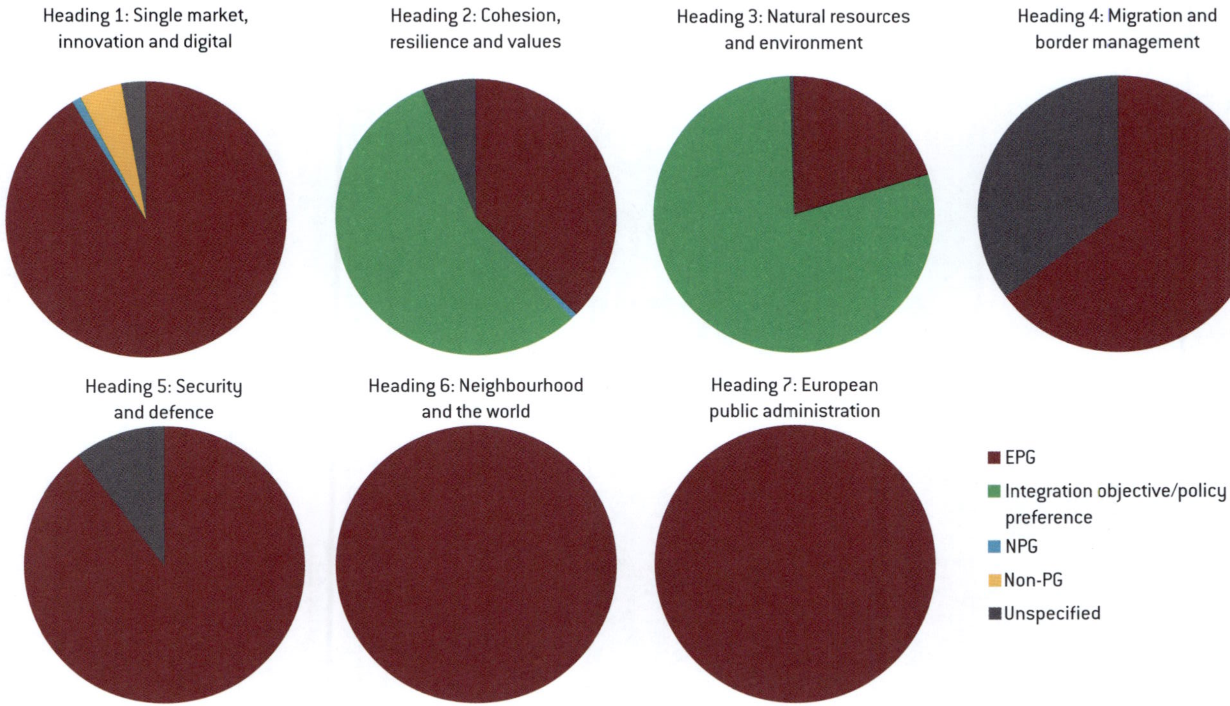

Source: Bruegel.

Figure 2: Overview of category allocation across different headings

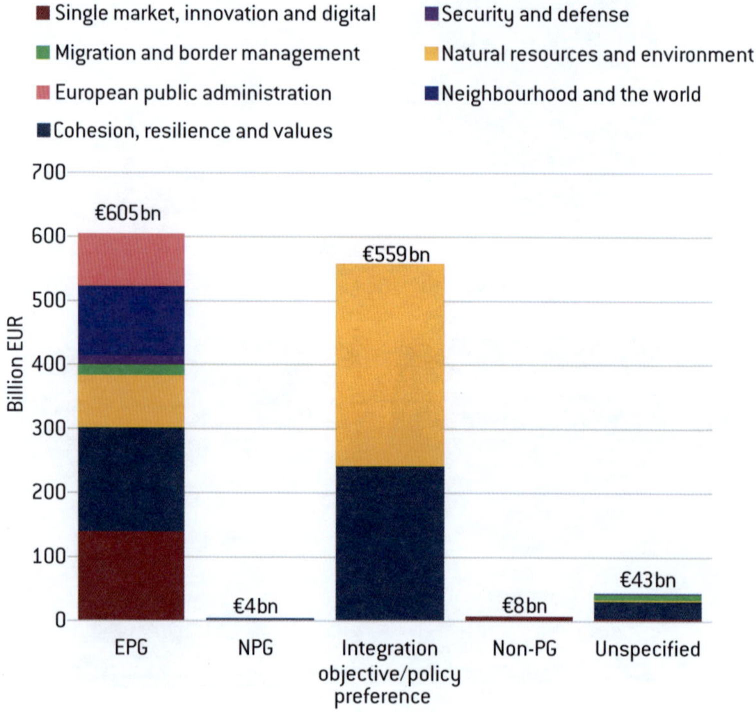

Source: Bruegel.

2.4 Assessing the EU budget's role in meeting additional public spending needs

Among the major challenges the EU will face in the years ahead - which will require significantly higher levels of spending than in the past - is the challenge of closing the EU's 'investment gap' as identified by Draghi (2024). Other types of expenditure will also be needed to support the provision of EPGs, even if they are not strictly classified as investment. This section analyses the funding needs, while chapter 4 examines the delivery method.

Many studies have quantified the EU's investment gaps, or the additional investment required to meet EU priorities in the next few years. Strictly speaking, some of the 'investment' considered in these studies does not correspond to investment in a traditional sense. For example, spending related to subsidising electric vehicles is often mentioned as a necessary investment to decarbonise the transport sector. However, this would be closer to industrial policy, rather than actual public investment, such as investment in public infrastructure. In this section, we examine the literature on the investment gap to identify important spending needs, while acknowledging that this also includes spending items that are not strictly related to investment.

We then examine the public share of overall spending needs and, within the public component, the respective contributions of EU and national spending. We map out two scenarios, both of which assume that the EU budget will help narrow spending gaps, but differ in their assumptions about the reallocation of current EU spending:

1. Maintaining current spending levels without reallocation: the size (as a share of GNI) and composition of current MFF spending remains unchanged in the 2028-2034 MFF with additional spending needs added on top;
2. Full reallocation to EPGs: the 2028-2034 MFF reallocates all spending items to EPGs, except for cohesion spending that facilitates redistribution between EU countries, as this cannot be nationalised. However, other current non-EPG spending would be transferred to national budgets. In this case, part of the additional spending is financed by reallocation, and thus the MFF increases by less than in the first case.

For both scenarios, we calculate the necessary increase in the EU budget as a share of GNI to meet spending needs.

2.5 Previous estimates of the total spending gap and the public sector's role

Various reports have estimated the EU's total investment needs, combining public and private contributions, at around 4 percent of GNI per year – often also including non-investment items. These estimates are uncertain, and reflect the areas covered and the timeframes used. Even more uncertainty arises when trying to estimate a public/private division of overall spending. Table 2 outlines total and public spending needs as calculated in different reports.

- Draghi (2024) suggested a plausible range for the public share between 20 percent and 50 percent[4], and noted that "*fiscal incentives to unlock private investment appear therefore necessary to finance the investment plan, in addition to direct government investment*", highlighting a higher overall fiscal burden. Draghi estimated the EU investment gap at €750 billion to €800 billion annually from 2025 to 2030. By assuming a public share of between 25 percent and 35 percent[5] this implies an additional annual public investment requirement equal to 1.1 percent to 1.6 percent of GNI.
- Bouabdallah *et al* (2024) calibrated the public share of investment

4 "*Direct public investment expenditures will also need to increase. They represent one fifth of the investment package in some scenarios, while accounting for a larger share – up to 50% – in others.*" (page 283 of Part B of Draghi, 2024). However, the report does not provide further details about the scenarios or sectors that require a public share higher than 20 percent, nor does it indicate the desirable average share of the public sector in total investment needs.

5 We consider a 25 percent to 35 percent range for the public share of total investment because Draghi (2024) suggested a 20 percent to 50 percent range (see footnote 4), excluding public incentives for private investment – an element Draghi (2024) deemed necessary. Therefore, we set the lower bound of the range at 25 percent. For the upper bound of the range, a 50 percent public contribution to all investment needs appears excessive based on other studies, such as Darvas and Wolff (2023) and Bouabdallah *et al* (2024). Consequently, we adopt a more conservative upper bound of 35 percent.

needs at 26 percent[6]. They noted the large uncertainty in investment-gap estimates and thus applied a range of +/- 20 percent around the total investment need, implying a public funding gap of between 0.8 percent and 1.2 percent of EU GNI per year. They also suggested an EU share at around 30 percent of public investment needs, implying an additional EU budget investment need of around 0.3 percent to 0.4 percent of GNI annually. This estimate is at the lower end of the suggested EU shares in the studies reviewed.

- Felbermayr and Pekanov (2024) estimated an upper ceiling for an EU budget that adequately finances EPGs at 3 percent of GNI, amounting to EU financing of around €540 billion per year.
- Studies on different investment need categories – the green transition (Pisani-Ferry and Tagliapietra, 2024) and defence spending (Burilkov and Wolff, 2025) – imply public financing between the ranges discussed above.

6 Numbers for Bouabdallah *et al* (2024) were read visually from the graph in the paper.

Table 2: Annual additional 'investment' needs

	Draghi (2024)	Bouabdallah *et al* (2024)	Felbermayr & Pekanov (2024)	Pisani-Ferry & Tagliapietra (2024); Burilkov and Wolff (2025)
Public share of total	25% - 35%	25%	-	Green transition: 25%-50%
EU share of public share	-	30%	-	
Additional annual total (private and public) investment needs, € billions				
	750-800	617-926	-	-
Additional annual public (national and EU) investment needs, € billions				
Green transition	113-158	117-175	-	86-172
Digital	38-53	11-17	-	-
Defence	13-18	21-32	-	-
Innovation	25-53	-	-	-
Infrastructure	-	-	-	-
Additional annual EU investment needs, € billions				
Green transition	-	32-48	-	-
Digital	-	11-17	-	-
Defence	-	3-4	180	125
Innovation	-	-	180	-
Infrastructure	-	-	180	-
Total public	190-280 (1.1% - 1.6% of EU GNI)	149-223 (0.8%-1.2% of EU GNI)		211-298 (1.2%-1.7% of EU GNI)
Total EU	-	47-70 (0.3%-0.4% of EU GNI)	540 (3.0% of EU GNI)	-

Source: Bruegel. Note: investment needs calculated over 2025-2030 in Draghi (2024) and 2025-2031 in Bouabdallah *et al* (2024). See footnote 5 for our calibration of the 25 percent to 35 percent public share based on Draghi (2024). Numbers for Bouabdallah *et al* (2024) are read visually from the graph in the paper and a +/-20 percent range is applied, as suggested by the authors. Felbermayr and Pekanov (2024) proposed their numbers in the context of the next EU budget. 'Infrastructure' in Felbermayr and Pekanov (2024) refers to the financing of pan-European infrastructure projects such as electricity, which are all classed under the green transition in other studies. Shares of EU GNI based on 2024 numbers at €17900 billion. Numbers are rounded and sums might thus not correspond to sub-components.

2.6 A more granular assessment of the EU budget's role in meeting spending needs

Most estimates reported in Table 2 are based on historical public financing patterns. However, given the evolving nature of spending needs, this approach is not the most appropriate for anticipating the role of public funding and, within it, the EU budget contribution.

In this section, we take a closer look at the EU's investment priorities and assess whether each investment item qualifies as a public good and, if so, whether it would benefit from EU-level financing.

This section focuses specifically on the green and digital transitions, given their strategic importance for the EU's future. The green transition assessment includes spending on international climate finance and innovation-related expenditures, which are often overlooked in evaluations of the EU's investment gap. We also discuss potential defence-related MFF spending needs, but lacking proper estimates, do not quantify this important spending item.

2.6.1 Additional spending needs: the green transition

To assess the green-transition related spending needs in different sectors, we rely on Baccianti (2022), Bizien *et al* (2024) and European Commission (2020b, 2023). We focus on five areas in particular: energy systems, buildings, transport, environmental measures and other sectors[7]. Notably, spending needs associated with climate adaptation are not included in these studies, and will not be covered, but we extend these studies by including possible EU-level spending on innovation and international climate finance.

From a public good perspective, climate protection ticks two important boxes: it is non-rival and it is not supplied at an adequate level without public intervention (Buti *et al*, 2023).

7 Investment needs for environmental protection are often not included in 'green investments,' which is why the overall investment gap might exceed the levels often cited in the public discourse.

Claeys and Steinbach (2024) argue that preferences across the EU are not always similar – resulting in a so-called trade-off EPG. In this context, we assess the degree to which green transition spending needs correspond to the EPG concept. Table 3 summarises these findings. We find a range between €134 billion and €142 billion annually for green spending needs that can be financed by the EU budget. This amounts to around 0.8 percent of GNI.

2.6.1.1 Energy systems

As the backbone of the green transition, energy systems are vitally important in electrifying the economy on a path to net-zero emissions. Energy-system investment needs can be separated into two main categories: grids and power generation.

Investment in grids can be categorised into three broad areas: distribution networks, transmission networks and interconnectors.

- Distribution networks are operated by private and public players across the EU, with public ownership at national or municipal level. They connect the end-consumer to the electricity network.
- Transmission networks transport energy over longer distances and are operated at national level.
- Interconnectors connect these national transmission networks across countries.

Most grid investments are expected to occur at the distribution level (Heussaff and Zachmann, 2025).

As distribution and transmission networks are already financed and operated locally, we see limited justification for EU involvement in financing this level of the grid. Current EU-level involvement is mostly connected to cohesion policy and is of a redistributive nature. As we have argued, cohesion policy should be viewed in the context of economic convergence as an important factor in the European integration process, but not as an EPG; rather, it can be categorised as an integration policy preference. Further helpful involvement of the EU is of a non-monetary nature, such as ensuring network interoperability (ECA, 2025).

We thus only categorise interconnectors as EPGs in the context of grid investment needs. ENTSO-E (2025) estimated the investment needs for interconnectors up to 2030 at €5 billion/year[8], which is also broadly in line with CIP (2025). Current investment under the Connecting Europe Facility – Energy provides about €1 billion/year[9] (Heussaff and Zachmann, 2025), meaning an investment gap related to interconnectors of €4 billion/year, or about 10 percent of total grid investment needs. Our estimate implies an EU contribution to public investment at around one-third, which is in line with the findings of Baccianti (2022), who estimated the share of public investment in grids at 30 percent.

For power generation, most investment is expected to come from the private sector. Baccianti (2022) estimated the public share of national and EU sources at 5 percent. Renewable energy subsidies will decrease over time and are currently largely national. The role of the EU could be to coordinate renewable deployment. This, in turn, can lead to efficiency gains in storage (Roth and Schill, 2023). The EU could also play a role by investing in R&D and supporting early-stage technologies; here, EU involvement would lead to efficiency gains and economies of scale. We assume the EU could contribute half of the 5 percent public investment share – thus an EU share of 2.5 percent.

In the medium and long terms, these investment needs are likely to change. As deployment of renewables and the electrification of the economy progress, the energy system will need to become more flexible. Part of this flexibility, through different storage options, will presumably change investment needs in relation to grid infrastructure,

8 ENTSO-E (2025) expects investment needs to gradually increase to €6 billion/year up to 2040 and to up to €13 billion/year up to 2050.

9 €5.8 billion from 2021-2027 under the current MMF.

while flexibility in power generation will be provided by, for example, a small number of gas power plants. These will need to be subsidised as they will not be profitable in their function as back-up power plants. This will presumably happen at national level and will not necessarily impact EU spending.

2.6.1.2 Buildings

Buildings require the largest amount of additional spending to meet the EU's 2030 climate targets. Most studies treat the need for investment in residential buildings, non-residential buildings and heating infrastructure separately.

From a public good perspective, spending in the building sector is difficult to assess. By reducing the carbon footprint of buildings and their impact on climate change, renovations have positive externalities. They are also provided at an insufficient level without government intervention (Keliauskaite *et al*, 2025). Renovation of buildings might therefore be classified as a public good. However, we consider it to be a national rather than European public good. With significant differences in countries' renovation needs, the efficiency effects of EU-level funding are unclear. In addition, there are possibly strong differences in preferences between EU countries. From a public good perspective, there is thus no clear rationale for the use of MFF resources for building renovations.

Building renovation subsidies can, if implemented properly, have redistributive effects, which we categorise as a policy preference. While not strictly a public good, public support for renovation might be necessary to avoid 'green backlash' and increase acceptance of climate policies in EU countries. In this respect, there is scope for the EU to become active – and it has. The Social Climate Fund, a policy instrument outside the MFF (see footnote 25), is aimed at redistributing a portion of emissions allowance revenues among EU countries to protect lower-income households (Jüngling *et al*, 2025).

2.6.1.3 Transport

The transport sector is one of the EU's main CO2 emitters. Accordingly, the spending needs are substantial. The transport sector can generally be divided into private and public – the former including passenger and commercial vehicles, while the latter refers to public transport.

Much of the need for investment in this category arises from the replacement of private internal combustion engine cars with electric vehicles (EVs). Replacement of old cars over time would happen anyway; the issue is to switch to more environmentally friendly cars at a rapid pace. To encourage the replacement, there is room for public intervention in the private transport sector. Most of this occurs in the form of subsidies at national level. While there are potential scale effects and efficiency gains from pooling these subsidies at EU level, this would be at odds with the different preferences of EU countries. We thus do not classify these subsidies as spending on an EPG.

Similarly to investment in buildings, EV subsidies have the potential for redistributive effects. A potential vehicle for EU-level coordination could again be the Social Climate Fund, aimed at subsidising EVs in an efficient way that reduces the impact on the most vulnerable.

Charging infrastructure is another aspect of the decarbonisation of private transport. It has clear scale effects and the potential for efficiency gains if coordinated at EU level. Bizien *et al* (2024) estimated the public charging infrastructure investment gap at €3.6 billion/year, which we classify as EPG spending.

While public transport infrastructure is typically considered to be a private good, public intervention might be needed in cross-border cases. We can thus separate investment needs into national public transport and the Trans-European Transport Network (TEN-T). While the former qualifies as a private good, the latter is clearly an EPG and should thus be financed fully by the EU.

Cohesion considerations could warrant EU involvement in public transport investment that does not involve cross-border investment. However, we disregard that here for the same reason as outlined above:

cohesion policy itself is not necessarily a public good but rather a policy preference.

2.6.1.4 Environmental measures

Environmental measures are textbook public goods. Without public intervention, environmental protection, sustainable resource management and investments in the circular economy would be severely undersupplied.

Generally, environmental protection has cross-border aspects – national governments potentially undersupply environmental protection by keeping it within their borders and disregard spillovers to neighbouring countries. Examples of environmental protection that can be considered EPGs include air quality protection, waste management including wastewater, soil and surface water protection and biodiversity. While some of these measures might seem like regional public goods, they also have global climate implications, which are often overlooked (Grabbe and Léry Moffat, 2024). Efficient resource management and the circular economy also have strong EPG characters because of cross-border aspects and scale effects.

Estimates in this spending category are difficult to capture. Existing works likely underestimate the spending need. As outlined in Fiore and Grabbe (2025), the annual financing gap for biodiversity alone may amount to €18 billion in the EU. In addition, any shortcoming in current spending earmarked for environmental protection and biodiversity might lead to increased spending needs in the future, thus widening the spending gap. As outlined in chapter 4, spending under the current CAP has been criticised for its limited contribution to environmental protection, while more than half of CAP spending was found to be harmful for biodiversity (WWF, 2024).

Baccianti (2022) suggested a 50 percent share of public spending on the circular economy, which we extrapolate to other environmental measures, while noting that more precise estimates are needed. We see a strong rationale for the EU to contribute fully to the public share in order to avoid potential undersupply by EU countries, and to produce scale effects where needed.

2.6.1.5 Other sectors

The decarbonisation of the real economy poses a major challenge because of the complex underlying dynamics and the differing needs of companies. This covers various areas including the decarbonisation of industry and services and the development of innovative technologies. These measures strengthen the EU's competitiveness globally and contribute to climate action.

Much of this spending will relate to the decarbonisation of production processes – for example, through the use of green hydrogen. Estimates presented by Baccianti (2022) and the European Commission (2023) mainly focus on industrial decarbonisation in the form of capital expenditure. Baccianti (2022) suggested a public share of 30 percent to 50 percent for the financing of the green transition in the industry sector. He argued that this would include, apart from investment grants, recurring subsidy payments. In our view, there is a strong rationale for fully centralising industrial subsidies at EU level to ensure a level playing field across the EU and to smooth out differences in national fiscal capacities. However, achieving this would require broad political consensus and substantial legislative change, which are unlikely in the near term. We therefore assume the continuation of the current institutional framework, in which industry-level subsidies for companies are provided at national level. Furthermore, investment grants that do not contribute to the financing of cross-border goods are better classified as spending on NPGs and should thus be financed at national level.

In line with the theory of public goods, public resources should be used where private investment in insufficient and results in an undersupply of climate action. This would apply to innovation related to the green transition. Areas here include R&D investment, support for early adoption of innovative clean technologies and the provision of financial de-risking tools to reduce the cost of capital for private investors (Pisani-Ferry and Tagliapietra, 2024). These areas would benefit from centralised EU involvement through the creation of economies of scale and efficiency gains. None of the studies we surveyed covers the financing of innovation. We thus add information from a literature review conducted by the European Parliamentary Research Service (Saulnier *et al*, 2025). This estimated the R&D investment gap for low-carbon innovation at between €10 billion and €26 billion per year, with a public component of €2 billion to €8 billion a year (25 percent to 30 percent). Given the substantial scale effects the EU could provide, the EU share of the public financing component could be 50 percent.

Table 3: Annual additional spending needs: green transition

	Baccianti (2022)	I4CE: Bizien *et al* (2024)	European Commission (2020b, 2023) / Saulnier *et al* (2025)	Bruegel estimates
Public share of total	54%	-	-	-
EU share of total	-	-	-	17%-25%
	Additional annual spending needs (public and private),€ billions (up to 2030)			Annual EU public spending needs, € billions
Energy systems	90	122	93	5-6
Grids	33	42	40	4
Power generation	57	80	53	1.3-2
Buildings	190	137	100	0
Heating	25	36	-	0
Residential	165	56	100	0
Non-residential		45	-	0
Other sectors	61	-	88-104	15-18
Industry	19	-	22	0
Tertiary	-	-	56	14
Innovation			10-26 (Saulnier *et al*, 2025)	1-4
Transport	109	147	205	33-37
Private	-	119	-	4
Public (national)	76	-	-	0
Public (TEN-T)	33	29	-	29-33
Environmental measures	42	-	130	65

Environmental protection	-	-	77	39
Resource management	42	-	38	19
Circular economy		-	15	8
SUM (total)	492 (2.7% of EU GNI)	616-632 (3.4-3.5% of EU GNI)		118-126 (0.7% of EU GNI)

Notes: Baccianti (2022) and the European Commission estimates show the annual spending gap for 2021-2030. The annual spending gap for Bizien *et al* (2024) is for 2024-2030. Commission based on Annex 1 in European Commission (2023) for energy systems, buildings, other sectors and transport and Table 1 in European Commission (2020b) final for environmental measures. Saulnier *et al* (2025) estimated the spending gap up to 2035. Shares of EU GNI based on 2024 numbers at €17900 billion. Numbers are rounded. The range for our estimate of the EU's percentage share in the total (as shown in the last column of the table) was calculated by dividing our lower estimate of EU spending needs (€118 billion) by the sum of the lower estimates from the three alternatives for each main category (€479 billion – for which we adjusted Baccianti's (2022) environmental measures estimate with the Commission's environmental protection estimate), and by dividing our higher estimate of EU spending needs (€126 billion) by the sum of the higher estimates from the three alternatives for each main category (€751 billion).

2.6.1.6 International climate finance

In addition to driving the green transition within the EU, supporting climate transition in developing economies is a critical but often overlooked aspect. The EU's role in international climate finance is essential for both reducing global emissions and from the strategic perspective of external action.

Bolton *et al* (2025) estimated that international climate finance needs will amount to $465 billion (about €410 billion) per year from 2025 to 2035, of which $124 billion (or €109 billion) would be provided by the public sectors of a coalition of willing countries, comprised of wealthy nations, including EU members. Based on this estimate, Bolton *et al* (2025) calculated that the EU, including both the EU budget and national contributions, would need to provide around $69 billion (or €61 billion) annually.

To estimate the *additional* spending needs, we need to subtract current spending levels from these amounts. In 2022, the EU and its members contributed €28.5 billion, implying a funding gap of about €32.5 billion. If we assume that 50 percent of this should be covered by the EU, balancing national preferences for foreign policy with the efficiency gains from EU-level spending, we arrive at an additional annual spending need to be met by the EU of around €16 billion.

Table 4: Annual additional spending needs: climate finance and green transition combined

	Bolton *et al* (2025)		Bruegel estimates
	Annual developed economies (private and public) spending needs, billions	Annual EU public (EU and national) spending needs, billions	Annual EU public spending gap, billions
International climate finance	410 (2.3% of EU GNI)	61 (0.3% of EU GNI)	16 (0.09% of EU GNI)
Other green transition spending			118-126 (0.7% of EU GNI)
SUM (total)			134-142 (0.8% of EU GNI)

Source: Bruegel. Note: international climate finance estimates show the annual investment gap for 2025-2035 and are based on Bolton *et al* (2025). Exchange rate assumed at $1.1343/€ (as of 5 May 2025, source: ECB). Shares of EU GNI based on 2024 value at €17900 billion. Numbers are rounded. Other green transition spending is from Table 3.

2.6.1.7 Additional spending needs – digital transition

To investigate the digital transition investment gap, we rely on European Commission estimates. Generally, the digital transition is not a public good - it is a private good. Investments that drive digitalisation, which primarily increase private sector productivity, are not considered a public good. This includes investment in high-performance computing (HPC), semiconductors, digital green technologies, cloud computing and artificial intelligence. Digital skills, which fall under the re-skilling of workers, can be seen as a private good.

Investment in communication networks, which are most undersupplied in rural areas, would either be spending on national public goods or policy preferences for integration. Communication networks can however also have aspects of cross-border infrastructure, such as the initiatives financed by CEF Digital (see annex 1), which we consider as an EPG. There is limited information available on how much of the investment gap in communication networks stems from cross-border considerations. Given estimates of a public share in telecommunications investment of about 30 percent (WIK-Consult, 2023), we estimate an EU contribution of about 10 percent.

Cybersecurity can be considered as a weakest-link public good. Because of its cross-border relevance, we classify it as an EPG. Spending associated with the European Commission's Next Generation Internet initiative is aimed at ensuring transparency, privacy and protection of data[10]. The protection of data and privacy rights can be considered a public good, and because of the cross-border nature of online activities can also be considered an EPG. Common European data spaces also have EPG characteristics: non-rival, positive externalities from research using public data and an undersupply by markets (Martens, 2024).

10 See European Commission, 'Next Generation Internet initiative,' https://digital-strategy.ec.europa.eu/en/policies/next-generation-internet-initiative.

Table 5: Additional annual spending needs: digital transition

	Audit supervisor	Bruegel estimates
	Additional annual spending needs (public and private), billions (up to 2030)	EU public spending needs
Communication networks	42	4
HPC, graphene and quantum	6	0
Cloud	11	0
AI	20	0
Digital green technologies	6	0
Cybersecurity	3	3
Digital innovation/data and Next Generation Internet	5	5
Semiconductor/photonics	17	0
Digital skills	9	0
Common European data spaces	3	3
Total	125 (0.7% of EU GNI)	15 (0.08% of EU GNI)

Source: Bruegel. Note: based on Table 3 in European Commission (2022) and denotes investment needs up to 2030. Shares of EU GNI based on 2024 numbers at €17900 billion. Numbers are rounded.

2.6.1.8 Additional spending needs – defence

While the EU budget cannot fund military expenditure directly, it can support the build-up of defence capabilities through industrial policy and R&D funding, and by incentivising joint procurement. Recent initiatives reflect a growing willingness among EU institutions and member states to expand such support via the EU budget. Wolff *et al* (2025) identified three main avenues via which EU facilities or regulations contribute to strengthening defence capacities:

1. Supply-side measures aimed at scaling up industrial capacity;
2. Incentivising cooperation in procurement of the most urgent defence products, potentially lowering costs;
3. Alleviation of national fiscal constraints, for example by offering loans to member states or allowing deviations from agreed fiscal adjustment paths.

The first two types of support are funded from the EU budget. An established part of the current MFF, the European Defence Fund (EDF) has a budget of €8 billion dedicated primarily to defence R&D. Several additional EU defence-related initiatives have been financed by repurposing MFF funds, including the European Defence Industry Reinforcement through Common Procurement Act (EDIRPA, Regulation (EU) 2023/2418) and the Act in Support of Ammunition Production (ASAP, Regulation (EU) 2023/1525).

EDIRPA is designed to cover the 'cooperation costs' associated with joint procurement projects involving multiple EU countries, thereby incentivising such cooperation. It has a €310 million envelope, €300 million of which is sourced from the EU budget[11] and €10 million from Norway. ASAP supports industrial policy measures to scale up ammunition production and is fully funded from the EU budget with an envelope of €500 million[12].

In addition, the European Commission proposed the European Defence Industry Programme (EDIP) in March 2024, which would expand ASAP to all defence industries (Wolff *et al*, 2025). The current proposal suggests an envelope of €1.5 billion for 2025-2027, which would also be funded under the current MFF's Heading 5.

11 According to the draft regulation (European Commission, 2022) this is sourced from Heading 5: Security and Defence. Note that the initial proposal foresaw an envelope of €500 million.

12 See Commission Implementing Decision, available at https://defence-industry-space.ec.europa.eu/document/download/5845b34d-bb2f-4381-aca3-ec9ff965f687_en.

However, industrial policy and research support alone are insufficient to meet the EU's defence capability needs. Security and defence are EPGs, but industrial and research policies can only enhance competitiveness and technological advancement in segments of the defence industry. The broader expenditure needs, particularly for military hardware and operational readiness, are vast and cannot be financed through the EU budget because of the Treaty restrictions.

While some estimates of overall defence investment needs have been made (Burilkov and Wolff, 2025), these typically focus on rearmament and equipment procurement, which cannot be funded by the industrial policy and research pillars of the EU budget.

The literature seems to lack a quantification of the specific spending needs to be financed by the EU budget in the form of industrial policy, R&D funding and procurement incentives. Such an analysis is beyond the scope of this Blueprint and therefore we do not provide an estimate for an EU contribution to defence spending needs. As a result, the EU budget spending needs we estimate in this chapter should be interpreted as a lower bound, since they exclude additional defence-related expenditures for which financing from the EU budget would be desirable.

2.7 An EPG-oriented EU budget

By combining the EU-funded additional spending needs we have estimated in this chapter, we arrive at €149 billion to €157 billion per year, or approximately 0.8 percent of GNI. These spending gap calculations are based on studies that typically assessed needs up to 2030. However, investment needs, particularly for the green transition, will not disappear and may even increase further (Pisani-Ferry and Tagliapietra, 2024), though the composition of this spending might change over time. The European Commission (2024) has also projected that green investment needs are set to increase until the net-zero target is reached in 2050. However, given the difficulty of extending our bottom-up approach into the future, we assume that the spending needs identified up to 2030 will remain for the rest of the 2028-2034 MFF period. Consequently, our results should be considered a lower-bound estimate of the MFF spending needs for that period.

A further issue in relation to the size of the 2028-2034 MFF is NextGenerationEU (NGEU) debt repayment, which is scheduled to begin in 2028. Over the 2028–2034 MFF period, interest and principal repayments on NGEU grant-related borrowing could amount to between €140 billion and €168 billion, or €20 billion to €24 billion annually, depending on whether the principal is repaid in equal euro amounts or equal share of GNI in 2028-2058 (Darvas and McCaffrey, 2024).

If NGEU is understood as a one-time response to the pandemic, providing additional EU resources rather than front-loading future EU spending, then its debt servicing costs should not be offset by reductions in other EU expenditure, particularly those focused on EPGs. Instead, these repayments should be added on top of the MFF, necessitating a further increase in its overall size.

In addition, fully covering the interest costs of current EU loans to Ukraine would require approximately €11.5 billion over the next MFF, or €1.6 billion annually (Darvas and McCaffrey, 2024). Combined, NGEU debt service and the Ukraine interest subsidy would result in additional EU spending of €152 billion to €180 billion over the 2028-2034 period, or €22 billion to €26 billion annually, corresponding to roughly 0.1 percent of EU GNI annually.

The annual additional 0.8 percent of GNI in EU spending that we estimate, and the 0.1 percent of GNI NGEU debt service/Ukraine interest subsidy, are substantial compared to the current MFF, which amounts to 1.1 percent of GNI. The additional amounts could be incorporated into the next MFF in two ways:

1. No reallocation from non-EPGs: the extra 0.9 percent of GNI EU spending annually would be added on top of the existing 1.1 percent GNI MFF, leading to a new MFF of 2.0 percent of GNI. This

would amount to a total of €2.9 trillion over the seven-year MFF[13].

2. Full reallocation of non-EPGs (except cohesion policy): Since cohesion policy has a cross-country redistribution objective and cannot be nationalised, only other non-EPG expenditures would be shifted to national budgets. We estimate these at 0.3 percent of GNI, resulting in an overall MFF spending ceiling of 1.7 percent of GNI, with MFF expenditures rising to €2.4 trillion in total over seven years.

These estimates represent the upper and lower bounds for an EU budget that would be large enough to finance the EPG part of additional spending needs. They do not include our proposed emergency fund (section 2.1), which could be activated in response to EU-wide spending emergencies, such as the COVID-19 pandemic or the 2015-2016 refugee crisis, thereby not requiring the diversion of resources away from EPGs within the MFF under exceptional circumstances (Buti *et al*, 2024). Nor do they include defence-related additional common spending[14].

Overall, the EU budget as currently set up is not big enough to achieve the EU's climate and digital goals. Even if non-EPG spending is deducted, a significant increase in EU expenditure will be necessary.

13 To calculate euro values, we used GNI based on the AMECO forecast (autumn 2024) up to 2026 and the European Commission's 2024 Ageing Report for long-term projections.

14 Some defence-related common spending could be included in the MFF, such as defence industrial policy and incentives for common procurement. Spending on military-related purchases, such as strategic enablers, may be more appropriately provided through an intergovernmental vehicle (Zettelmeyer *et al*, 2025). We did not include defence-related spending needs in our calculation because of the lack of availability of studies quantifying the spending gaps and the possible role of the EU in filling these gaps.

3 EU budget revenues and the search for new sources

3.1 Context

EU budget revenues, referred to as 'own resources' in the Treaty on the Functioning of the European Union (TFEU, Article 311)[15], are primarily composed of contributions from member states, as the EU lacks the authority to design and implement its own revenue collection mechanisms. Most of these contributions are calculated statistically, based in particular on EU member state gross national income (GNI) and value-added tax (VAT) revenues. Revenues arising from the implementation of a common EU policy, such as customs duties collected under the EU's common trade policy, are typically referred to as 'genuine own resources'. However, even these genuine own resources are collected by national administrations, as the EU does not have its own collection agencies for customs duties or taxes.

Given that the term 'own resources' is somewhat misleading – most of these revenues are not directly 'owned' by the EU but are instead allocated by member states – we refer to them as 'EU budget revenues' throughout this chapter. This chapter reviews proposals for new EU budget revenue resources to finance new EU spending, repay the EU borrowing that has financed NextGeneration EU (NGEU) grants and fund the interest subsidy for Ukraine (chapter 2).

15 'Own resources' refers to all revenue streams assigned to the EU budget by the Own Resources Decision (ORD, Council Decision 2020/2053), a special legislative procedure pursuant to Article 311 that requires unanimity of EU countries. Other sources such as proceeds from fines resulting from breaching EU laws are not designated in the ORD and are not called 'own resources'.

EU finances are governed by various ceilings established in two main laws. The Own Resources Decision (ORD) sets out the financing system of the EU budget, including the overall ceilings on the amounts that can be allocated. It is adopted unanimously by the EU governments and must be ratified by all EU countries in line with their national constitutional requirements. The ORD does not have a fixed end date, but remains in force until a new decision replaces it.

The second main law is the Council regulation on the Multiannual Financial Framework (MFF; most recently: Council Regulation (EU, Euratom) 2020/2093 of 17 December 2020). This also requires unanimous adoption by EU countries but not national ratification, and its adoption is subject to the consent of the European Parliament. The MFF must cover a period of at least five years, though since 1993, each framework has spanned seven years. It sets ceilings on EU spending, within the limits of the ORD, both for the overall seven-year period and for the main categories of spending, known as headings (chapter 2). Two types of ceiling are applied to EU spending: commitments (a reservation to cover future payments) and payments (the actual amounts paid out).

The 2020 ORD (Council Decision 2020/2053) raised the EU budget's own resources ceiling (ie the maximum amount EU countries could be asked to contribute to the EU budget) by an additional 0.6 percent of EU GNI in each of the 38 years from 2021 to 2058, to cover NGEU-related liabilities. This extra resource cannot be allocated to other purposes[16]. However, the European Parliament, the Council of the EU

16 Darvas and McCaffrey (2024) estimated that this additional revenue ceiling is 9.5 times greater than the anticipated cost of NGEU grant-related interest and principal repayments.

and the European Commission[17] said in 2020 they wanted to offset the increases in the GNI-based contributions needed for the repayment of NGEU debt, and have instead proposed that sufficient new EU budget revenues should be introduced.

Introducing additional EU budget revenues has already proved challenging. European Commission proposals in 2021 triggered a lively debate but did not lead to any agreement. The European Parliament in May 2023 made a non-binding proposal for new revenue resources, followed by a revised Commission proposal a few months later. The European Parliament then approved the Commission's revised proposal, but at time of writing it still awaits Council decision, and negotiations appear to be at a standstill.

We next set out a brief overview of EU budget revenues, followed by a discussion of core principles in the search for new EU budget revenues. We then examine the Commission's proposals and alternative suggestions. Finally, we describe the extent of and rationale for revenue correction mechanisms ('rebates'), before concluding.

3.2 EU budget revenues from 2000-2023

The main source of revenue for the EU budget since 2000 has been the GNI-based contribution (Figure 3), which reached €98 billion in 2023. The next two largest revenue sources, customs duties and VAT-based revenues, each contributed approximately €22 billion in 2023. A levy on non-recycled plastic waste, introduced at the start of 2021, added €7 billion. The United Kingdom provided an additional €9 billion as part of the Brexit settlement, though this revenue will decline gradually. Other revenues (administrative revenues, financial revenues, default interest

17 2020 Interinstitutional Agreement between the between the European Parliament, the Council of the European Union and the European Commission on budgetary discipline, on cooperation in budgetary matters and on sound financial management, as well as on new own resources. See points E and F of the Preamble of Annex II at https://eur-lex.europa.eu/eli/agree_interinstit/2020/1222/oj#ntr1-LI2020433EN.01002801-E0001.

and fines, and the surplus from the previous year) amounted to €22 billion. Meanwhile, EU borrowing has financed NGEU spending.

Figure 3: EU annual budget revenues, % GNI, 2000-2023

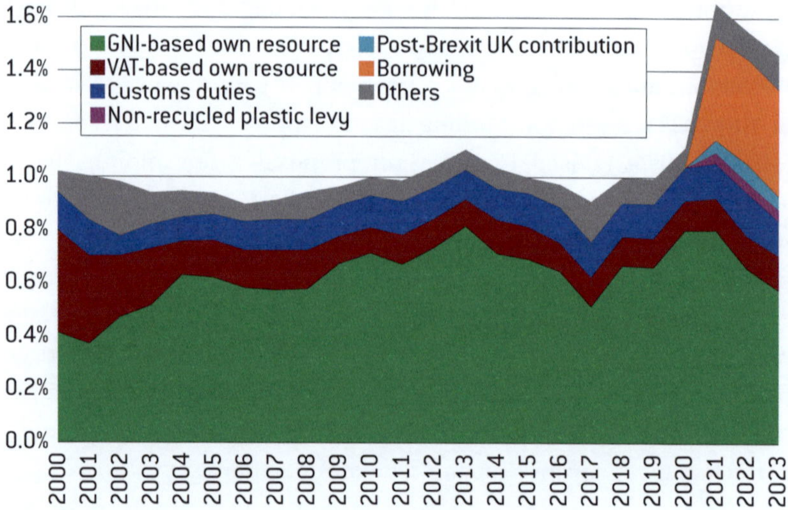

Source: Bruegel based on European Commission and adopted EU annual budgets.

3.3 EU budget revenues: main principles

The case for expanding the sources of revenue that flow into the EU budget is less straightforward than it initially seems. First, raising additional revenue beyond the GNI-based contribution will generally not raise EU budget revenue, only change its composition (section 3.3.1). Second, any increase in EU budget revenue represents an opportunity cost to member-state budgets, even if it is financed from additional genuine own resources (section 3.3.2). Furthermore, raising additional own resources will normally have distributional implications (section 3.3.3). Nevertheless, there are good reasons to shift the budget away from GNI-based contributions towards genuine own resources (section 3.3.4).

3.3.1 New EU budget revenues do not necessarily generate additional resources

The ORD defines GNI-based contributions as a balancing item to cover the gap between actual EU spending within the budget ceiling (currently about 1.1 percent of GDP) and all other revenue sources (Figure 3)[18]. Consequently, until a new ORD is agreed, raising additional revenue at the margin, by changing the parameters of existing revenue sources or introducing new ones, will merely reduce GNI-based contributions, leaving total revenue unchanged.

For example, when the non-recycled plastic levy was introduced as a new revenue source for the 2021-2027 Multiannual Financial Framework (MFF), the overall expenditure ceiling was not increased and so the levy did not increase total EU budget revenues. Instead, EU countries contributed through the new levy while reducing their GNI-based contributions by an equivalent amount. Because the levy's cross-country distribution differs from the GNI distribution (Table 6), its introduction changed the national contributions to the EU budget.

For example, Germany recycles a relatively large share of its plastic waste and, as a result, saved €400 million in EU budget contributions in 2023: Germany paid €1.4 billion based on the plastic levy but would have paid €1.8 billion in the absence of the levy, as the €7 billion in EU budget revenue from the levy in 2023 would then have been allocated according to GNI. In contrast, France recycles relatively less, and the levy increased its contribution to the EU budget by €350 million in 2023: France paid €1.56 billion under the levy, but would have paid only €1.21

18 Since 1988, the ORD has defined a theoretical 'own resources ceiling' (currently at 1.4 percent of GNI), referring to the maximum amount that could be collected for the EU budget. The difference between the own resources ceiling and the MFF's expenditure ceiling (currently approximately 1.1 percent of GNI) is often referred to as a 'safety margin' or 'budgetary headroom'. It ensures that the EU can meet its financial obligations, such as servicing debt from borrowing used to finance loans to Ukraine. This budgetary headroom has never been used, while actual expenditure has often fallen slightly short of the expenditure ceiling. Thus, actual annual expenditures have determined the amount of EU budget revenues collected.

billion if, in the absence of the levy, the €7 billion had been allocated according to GNI. It is also worth emphasising that the levy has a beneficial side effect by encouraging stronger national-level recycling policies (for further discussion, see section 3.3.4).

Thus, without increasing the EU budget expenditure ceiling, introducing new revenue sources would reduce GNI-based contributions without increasing the total revenue intake, while altering the distribution of contributions across countries and potentially advancing certain EU policy objectives, such as promoting recycling in the case of the plastic waste levy.

3.3.2 Any expansion of the EU budget represents an opportunity cost to member states' budgets

If additional EU revenues enable increased budget expenditures, they will inevitably have an opportunity cost for EU countries, because those additional revenues could have been directed to national budgets rather than the EU budget. This is most obvious if the additional revenues are based on existing revenue sources, such as the VAT or GNI-based contributions, since these would be directly at the expense of member-state budgets. But the same is true even when such revenues could not have been raised by EU members individually (ie raising them requires coordination or they must be raised at EU level, such as customs duties), as EU members could agree to raise such resources collectively and redistribute them to national budgets.

3.3.3 Any new EU budget revenue source changes the distribution of contributions to the budget

The cross-country distribution of alternative revenue sources differs from the distribution of GNI across countries (Table 6; see also the German and French examples in section 3.3.1 in relation to the plastic waste levy). Therefore, choices over how any new EU budget revenue sources are shared between countries affect the distribution of contributions across member states.

3.3.4 Arguments for shifting from GNI-based contributions to genuine own resources

Levies on activities for which the EU is competent belong to the EU collectively. There is greater political legitimacy in directing these revenues to the EU budget than in directing national VAT or GNI shares to the EU budget (Monti *et al*, 2017). Thus, as long as genuine own resources remain below the payment ceiling (requiring a top-up in the form of GNI-based contributions), they should arguably be allocated to the EU budget in their entirety (apart from a collection fee). This is not the case currently. For example, competition policy fines go directly to the EU budget, but EU countries keep 25 percent of customs duties – much more than can be justified as compensation for collection costs.

Meanwhile, the EU's heavy reliance on GNI-based contributions has entrenched a 'culture of net balances', with EU countries focusing narrowly on the difference between what they contribute to and receive from the EU budget (European Commission, 2021a; Buti *et al*, 2024). This makes net contributors reluctant to support budget expansion, fearing that their taxpayers are subsidising others, overlooking the private and collective benefits of common EU spending.

Shifting to genuine own resources, with EU countries acting only as revenue collectors, could help counter this mindset, but is unlikely to eliminate it entirely. Even with genuine own resources, it remains easy for national politicians and the public to aggregate all flows to the EU budget and judge their own position in net terms.

EU-level collection of EU revenues could further weaken the link, but might be seen as violating the subsidiarity principle (under which new tasks should not be allocated to EU level when they can arguably be performed at national level) and the fundamental importance of taxation to national sovereignty. Creating, say, an EU tax agency would face both political resistance and technical hurdles[19].

Another justification for new types of EU budget revenues is that they could have positive impacts beyond revenue generation. For instance, the non-recycled plastic waste levy encourages recycling, benefitting the environment and aligning with EU goals. Environment-related EU revenues could have similar effects. The EU emissions trading system (ETS), for example, generates revenue through the auctioning of emission allowances but is also the EU's main tool for reducing greenhouse gas emissions, by putting a price on carbon. Similarly, the carbon border adjustment mechanism (CBAM) aims to prevent carbon leakage by imposing a carbon price on certain imports, thereby levelling the playing field for EU producers and encouraging decarbonisation globally. Both instruments, though currently not feeding into the EU budget, reinforce the EU's climate objectives while creating potential sources of revenues that are closely tied to policy goals. However, as with other behavioural taxes, there is an inherent trade-off: the more effective these instruments are at changing behaviour and reducing emissions, the less revenue they will ultimately generate.

To summarise: the main reason for introducing new EU budget revenues should not be solely revenue generation, but rather shifting the focus away from net balances in the EU budget, and advancing the EU's overarching objectives.

3.3.5 Avoiding regressive EU budget contributions

Finally, in thinking about EU budget revenues, the relative prosperity and capacity to contribute of each EU country must be taken into account, along with the need to correct regressive elements in the current budget revenue system. These points are included explicitly in Protocol No. 28 on Economic, Social, and Territorial Cohesion in the TFEU. They imply

19 National tax administrations are often among the most efficient national institutions, further justifying the reliance on them, though this does not mean that an EU tax administration would be inefficient.

that any new proposals for EU budget revenues should not be regressive. If regressive elements are present, corrective mechanisms should be proposed to mitigate their impact.

3.4 European Commission proposals for new EU budget revenues

The European Commission in 2021 proposed three new EU budget revenue sources: from the EU carbon border adjustment mechanism (CBAM), emission trading system (ETS) and Pillar One of the OECD/G20-led international tax agreement (European Commission, 2021b). Responding to suggestions from European Parliament (2023), which provided a long list of potential new revenue sources, the European Commission (2023b) adjusted these proposals, resulting in the following set of proposals:

- Channelling 75 percent of CBAM revenues to the EU budget (or about €1.5 billion/year); CBAM is in force since October 2023 but will generate resources only from 2026;
- 30 percent of revenues (about €19 billion/year) from sales of carbon allowances from the two parallel EU ETSs: ETS1 (the ETS in place since 2005, which covers mainly industrial emissions) and ETS2, which will cover mainly emissions from buildings and road transport, and which is at time of writing being phased in. The Commission proposed to channel ETS1 revenues from 2024 and ETS2 revenues from 2028;
- Business in Europe: Framework for Income Taxation (BEFIT), a proposal to reboot negotiations on a common EU approach to taxation of corporate profits, which was tabled in September 2023 with an own resources element to be added later (European Commission, 2023c);
- A contribution based on national accounts data on corporate profits (which could raise EU budget revenues of between €3 billion to €16 billion per year, depending on the call rate). This would be a temporary own resource acting as a proxy to corporate income tax

revenue, until BEFIT becomes operational;

- A new resource based on a re-allocation of taxing rights under Pillar One of the OECD/G20-led agreement among 138 countries (See Box 1); the Commission proposed to channel 15 percent of such revenues to the EU budget. Based on country-specific estimates by Barake and Le Pouhaër (2024), we calculate the annual EU budget revenue from this resource at a limited €0.5 billion/year[20]. However, Pillar One has been delayed and is highly unlikely to be concluded, especially after the November 2024 US election.

Among these proposals, the own resources based on CBAM, the ETS and the temporary statistical own resource tied to corporate profits are awaiting further decisions. Other own-resource ideas have not been developed into formal proposals. The process is lagging behind schedule[21], which planned for the implementation of the Commission's 2021 proposals by 1 January 2023.

Both the CBAM and the ETS may not generate long-term revenue, since exporting countries might adopt their own carbon taxes instead of letting the European Union collect it in the case of CBAM, while the EU's 2050 net-zero target will eliminate most new emissions and thus

20 Barake and Le Pouhaër (2024) estimated that 21 EU countries would see net tax-revenue gains under the Pillar One agreement, while Bulgaria, Cyprus, Hungary, Ireland, Luxembourg and Malta would face losses when considering all countries, not just those in the Inclusive Framework. The total tax revenue gains for the 21 benefiting countries are estimated to be between €3.65 billion and €3.88 billion in 2025. Applying a 15 percent share to these figures suggests that the EU budget could receive between €547 million and €583 million in revenue. These amounts are slightly lower when only Inclusive Framework countries are taken into account.

21 See European Parliamentary Research Service, 'Roadmap to the introduction of new own resources', undated, https://epthinktank.eu/2023/06/19/reform-of-the-eu-system-of-own-resources-state-of-play/roadmap_for_new-own-resources-socme_timeline_timeline/.

ETS revenues[22]. Nevertheless, in the coming years, including during the 2028-2034 MFF, these mechanisms will likely generate significant revenues and would generate even more for the EU budget if EU members were to keep only (small) collection costs, instead of the proposed large 25 percent to 30 percent share of these revenues.

The scope of CBAM could be widened to include additional sectors and products within the production chain. Such a widened scope could significantly increase the revenues generated by this resource. A major opportunity for this should come with the European Commission's report on the inclusion of value chain products within the scope of CBAM, due by the end of 2025, as required by Article 30(3) of the CBAM Regulation (Regulation (EU) 2023/956).

Since carbon pricing remains unpopular when its costs are directly borne by households, a political commitment has been made to channel the allocation of ETS revenues to social compensation and redistribution. ETS1 revenues are already channelled to two EU funds outside the MFF, the Innovation Fund[23] and the Modernisation Fund[24]. ETS2 revenues, plus additional ETS1 revenues, will be channelled to the

22 For 2030, Pisani-Ferry and Tagliapietra (2024) estimated ETS revenues of €65 billion, assuming an ETS carbon price of €75 and an ETS2 carbon price of €45. Of this, €50 billion would go to EU countries and €15 billion to the EU budget. If carbon prices rise to €130 for ETS and €100 for ETS2 by 2030, total revenues would reach €134 billion, with €100 billion accruing to member countries and €34 billion to the EU budget.

23 The Innovation Fund supports highly innovative clean technologies in areas such as energy-intensive industries, renewables, energy storage, net-zero mobility and buildings, hydrogen and carbon capture, use and storage. It is funded with 530 million ETS allowances, generating total revenues of €40 billion from 2020 to 2030, assuming a carbon price of €75.

24 The Modernisation Fund supports the modernisation of energy systems and improvements in energy efficiency in 13 lower-income EU countries. It is financed through revenues from the auctioning of 2 percent of the total ETS allowances for 2021–2030. Assuming a carbon price of €75, the fund's total revenues are estimated at €57 billion for the period.

Social Climate Fund[25], which is also outside the MFF.

Meanwhile, while BEFIT is unlikely to achieve consensus in the near future, a new revenue source based on corporate income has many positive features. First, it would maintain pressure on EU countries to move into the direction of corporate income tax harmonisation. Second, it would more equitably distribute the burden of EU budget revenues among EU countries. While eastern European countries are relatively more affected by CBAM and ETS, western economies and small, open economies would account for greater shares of contributions under this new resource (see annex 1). This would be particularly true for Ireland and Luxembourg, which currently benefit from the establishment of a 15 percent global minimum effective tax and the lack of progress on Pillar One (which would have otherwise reallocated part of their revenues to other countries, in addition to the EU own resource mechanism linked to Pillar One).

25 The Social Climate Fund was established alongside ETS2 to support vulnerable groups most affected by energy and transport poverty. It focuses on areas such as energy efficiency, building renovations, clean heating and cooling, integration of renewable energy, zero- and low-emission mobility solutions and temporary direct income support. The fund will draw revenues from the auctioning of allowances under ETS2, along with 50 million allowances from ETS1. Total revenues are expected to reach €65 billion between 2026 and 2032. Combined with a mandatory 25 percent contribution from EU countries, the fund is projected to mobilise at least €86.7 billion during this period.

Table 6: Distribution of current and prospective own resources (% share by country for each revenue resource)

	Existing EU budget revenues in 2021-2023						Prospective EU budget revenues		
	GNI-based own resource	VAT-based own resource	Customs duties	Plastic levy	ETS 1	ETS 2	Corporate profits	Pillar One of OECD agreement	Defence spending shortfall levy
Germany	25.36	24.23	20.33	21.44	24.20	23.73	22.37	34.41	31.48
France	17.32	18.59	9.30	21.23	6.62	15.61	13.84	23.95	4.17
Italy	12.33	11.54	10.68	12.34	11.42	13.19	14.42	9.75	14.35
Spain	8.47	9.18	8.53	8.58	10.90	8.27	8.54	8.60	13.47
Netherlands	5.92	6.16	15.40	3.17	4.05	4.18	6.43	2.85	5.90
Poland	3.95	4.58	5.32	7.54	16.02	8.11	4.85	1.09	---
Sweden	3.57	3.52	2.62	1.64	0.98	1.36	2.65	1.86	0.96
Belgium	3.46	3.28	10.83	2.41	2.31	3.84	3.51	0.76	5.29
Austria	2.80	3.01	1.16	2.48	1.32	2.67	2.63	2.64	5.55
Denmark	2.34	2.11	1.85	1.94	1.27	1.19	2.06	2.63	0.61
Portugal	1.49	1.71	1.14	2.73	2.24	1.58	1.43	1.17	2.78
Czechia	1.67	1.65	1.67	1.00	1.60	2.53	2.05	0.10	2.15
Ireland	2.22	1.63	2.03	2.74	0.53	1.54	5.03	---	7.55
Finland	1.73	1.51	0.83	1.13	1.80	1.18	1.53	8.06	1.29
Romania	1.73	1.38	1.19	2.73	1.05	2.50	2.25	0.58	0.82
Greece	1.27	1.22	1.75	0.97	4.43	1.62	1.58	0.81	---

Hungary	1.04	1.04	1.30	3.10	1.83	1.84	1.14	---	0.22
Slovakia	0.68	0.66	0.92	0.50	0.95	1.00	0.80	0.26	0.82
Bulgaria	0.49	0.57	0.70	0.54	3.39	0.91	0.58	---	0.43
Croatia	0.40	0.47	0.25	0.32	0.44	0.68	0.38	0.16	0.45
Slovenia	0.36	0.40	0.79	0.22	0.57	0.54	0.32	0.02	0.42
Luxembourg	0.34	0.39	0.07	0.20	0.01	0.56	0.45	---	1.00
Lithuania	0.38	0.38	0.57	0.24	0.28	0.54	0.42	0.10	---
Latvia	0.23	0.25	0.26	0.24	0.25	0.32	0.20	0.10	---
Estonia	0.21	0.24	0.22	0.35	1.06	0.26	0.21	0.08	---
Cyprus	0.15	0.18	0.18	0.07	0.33	0.19	0.19	---	0.02
Malta	0.09	0.11	0.10	0.14	0.13	0.06	0.15	---	0.27
Total	100.00	100.00	100.00	100.00	100.00	100.00	100.00	100.00	100.00

Source: Bruegel based on (1) European Commission budget execution data for the four current own resources; (2) average 2024-2030 ETS1 revenue projections from https://carbonmarketwatch.org/eu-ets-revenue-simulator/, which do not include allowances to the Modernisation Fund, the Innovation Fund and the Social Climate Fund; (3) ETS2 revenue projections from Table 8 of Graichen and Ludig (2024); (4) gross operating surplus data in 2021-2023 from Eurostat's 'GDP and main components (output, expenditure and income) [nama_10_gdp]' dataset; (5) data column 5 from Table 4 in Barake and Le Pouhaër (2024), which covers all countries, not just those in the Inclusive Framework (see Box 1); (6) Eurostat's General government expenditure by function (COFOG) [gov_10a_exp] and GDP and main components (output, expenditure and income) [nama_10_gdp] datasets. Note: countries are ordered based on their contributions to GNI-based EU budget revenues. CBAM is excluded from the analysis because of the unavailability of cross-country distribution estimates. For Pillar One of the OECD tax agreement, we assumed the six EU countries that would face net tax revenue losses, according to Barake and Le Pouhaër (2024), would not contribute. The defence spending shortfall levy is introduced in section 5.6 of this chapter. The numbers in the last column of the table correspond to a 2 percent of GDP defence spending threshold and use 2023 data for the calculations.

Box 1: The OECD/G20 Inclusive Framework on Base Erosion and Profit Shifting

In October 2021, 138 member countries of the OECD/G20 Inclusive Framework on Base Erosion and Profit Shifting agreed on a so-called 'Two-Pillar Solution' to address the tax challenges arising from the digitalisation of the economy.

Pillar One provides for the reallocation of a portion of excess profits of the largest multinational enterprises (MNEs) (those with revenues above €2 billion) to market countries, based on a new nexus rule tied to revenue thresholds in the countries where they operate. In essence, a quarter of the excess profits – defined as profits exceeding 10 percent of sales – will be reallocated to the countries where goods are sold and services are provided. Implementing Pillar One requires a Multilateral Convention, which has not been finalised and may never be signed or ratified.

Pillar Two establishes common rules to ensure that MNEs with revenues above €750 million pay an effective minimum tax rate of at least 15 percent in the countries where they operate. The minimum tax (the Global Anti-Base Erosion, or GloBE, rules) is implemented through an interlocking mechanism. Under this system, the tax is collected:

1. In the country where the MNE is headquartered (via the Income Inclusion Rule),
2. In the country where the profit is generated (via the Qualified Minimum Top-Up Tax), or
3. In the market countries where goods and services are provided, if the income remains untaxed under the first two rules (via the Under-Taxed Profit Rule, UTPR).

See: https://www.oecd.org/newsroom/138-countries-and-jurisdictions-agree-historic-milestone-to-implement-global-tax-deal.htm.

3.5 Other own resources proposals

Politicians and academics are never short on ideas for new taxes. Proposals, including from the European Parliament (2023) vary from sectoral levies to financial transaction taxes. They are not necessarily consistent, and can mix genuine own resources and statistically based contributions. Thöne (2024) classified proposals into the following categories: 1) financial sector taxation, 2) climate taxation, 3) statistically based, 4) corporate taxation and 5) wealth taxation. Kubeková *et al* (2024) explored options to boost other revenues.

3.5.1 Financial sector taxation

The financial sector is often targeted by proposals for new EU budget revenues, ranging from excise duties on share buybacks, taxes on crypto activities or extending VAT on financial services. A financial transactions tax (FTT) is often put forward, despite the failure to make progress on it at EU level, even as an enhanced cooperation project. This suggests that political capital would be better invested in identifying other EU budget revenues than the FTT.

3.5.2 Climate taxation

The debate on climate-related taxation has led to various proposals for new EU budget revenues, including a tax on electricity, additional charges on road transportation and levies on aviation and shipping. However, given the Commission's prioritisation of CBAM and ETS-related revenues in its proposals, the likelihood of additional carbon-related taxes being adopted appears low.

An exception could be the expansion of carbon taxation on shipping[26] and aviation. This would reinforce EU climate leadership

26 On 11 April 2025, the International Maritime Organisation agreed a binding greenhouse gas reduction framework. However, the agreed pricing mechanism cannot be assimilated to a tax mechanism and should be seen only as an intermediate step.

in sectors that are traditionally difficult to regulate. Together, these industries account for approximately 6 percent of global carbon emissions and currently face minimal or no carbon taxation. Their international nature has allowed them to evade national carbon pricing schemes, making them a logical focus for EU-level action. While both sectors are gradually being integrated into the EU ETS, significant exemptions still apply. For instance, in aviation, only flights within the European Economic Area are covered, while similar limitations exist for shipping. Expanding the EU ETS to fully encompass these sectors could help bridge the gap.

Alternatively, the EU could consider targeted taxation measures, such as a levy on aviation fuel (kerosene tax), a per-flight tax or a ticket tax on passengers. Some EU countries have already introduced such measures, providing a precedent for broader EU-level implementation.

Levies on aviation are of two broad types: fuel levies and ticket levies. Fuel levies are direct taxes on the fuel loaded for a flight. Ticket levies, or air passenger levies, are fixed fees added directly to ticket prices. Ticket levies can further be differentiated based on whether the tax is a fixed fee (sometimes called a "trip tax"; Keen and Strand, 2007), or whether the tax is proportional to the value of the ticket. Most current ticket taxes are trip taxes. Landau (2004) proposed the taxation of air corridors, but this is less discussed in the literature[27].

While fuel taxes relate closely to quantities of fuel consumed and therefore to CO2 emissions, this is less the case with ticket levies, although there are mechanisms to better align ticket levies with emissions intensity. For instance, fees can be adjusted depending on the destination, with higher fees for emissions-heavy long-distance travel. Fees can also be adjusted based on the ability of passengers to

27 Belgium, for example, introduced an aviation tax in 2022, applying a levy per passenger: €10 per passenger where the final destination is less than 500km distant; €2 per passenger where the final destination is more than 500km and located inside the European Economic Area (EEA), the UK or Switzerland; and €4 per passenger where the final destination is outside of the EEA, the UK or Switzerland

pay by differentiating the tax by ticket class (economy vs business and first class) – also reflecting the amount of space used within the plane and the weight carried.

Agriculture, meanwhile, accounts for about a quarter of greenhouse gas emissions, but is exempt from emissions taxation. The introduction of such taxes would support the sector's green transition. Agriculture taxes are planned, for example, in Denmark, alongside certain subsidies to foster environmental goals, such as afforestation and reduced use of fertilisers (Box 2). Ultimately, the agricultural sector should be included in the ETS, which would help level the playing field across EU farms and could serve as the basis for a new source of EU budget revenue.

Box 2: The 'Agreement on a Green Denmark' and its carbon tax on agriculture

In 2024, Denmark proposed a system for pricing farm greenhouse gas emissions. It will introduce taxes on:

- Emissions from livestock from 2030, starting at DKK 300 (around €40) per tonne of carbon dioxide equivalent (CO_2e), increasing to 750 DKK (around €100) per tonne CO_2e in 2035;
- Emissions from drained peatlands in agricultural use of DKK 40 (around €5) per tonne CO_2e in 2028.

The tax on livestock will receive a base deduction of 60 percent, which is aimed to provide an incentive to use technological solutions at the margin and to limit the increase in production costs. The corresponding agreement also foresees subsidies for:

- 250,000 hectares of afforestation and rewetting of 140,000 hectares of drained peatlands currently used for agriculture;
- Reducing the use of fertiliser on fields by restructuring direct payments provided through the CAP at €100 per tonne CO_2e from 2028;
- The storage of biochar produced by pyrolysis.

The effects of the agreement are estimated to increase prices by around 1 percent with a decline in production of around 4 percent in 2030. The estimated reduction of Danish emissions is 1.8 million tonnes of CO2e in 2030.

Sources: Danish Ministry of Climate, Energy and Utilities, 'Effektvurderinger af klimaløsning for landbruget mv.', 28 June 2024, https://oem.dk/media/0nnjpesh/3-effektvurderinger-af-klimaloesning-for-landbruget-mv_-a.pdf; 'Denmark's position on an EU ETS for agriculture – incentives for a sustainable, climate-friendly and competitive agricultural production in the EU', undated, https://www.ft.dk/samling/20241/almdel/euu/bilag/234/2969188.pdf; Expert Group for a Green Tax Reform (2024).

3.5.3 Statistically based own resources

Building on the precedent set by the plastic waste levy, successfully introduced in 2021 (section 3.2), some proposals have suggested further waste-related statistical resources, based on food waste, e-waste or other waste beyond plastic packaging.

Beyond environmental considerations, other statistical-based revenue proposals have emerged. The European Parliament (2023) proposed a levy linked to countries' gender pay gaps and a 'fair border mechanism,' which would impose a levy on imported goods and services when workers in exporting countries are paid below international poverty thresholds.

These measures seek to advance policy objectives while generating revenue. However, they require further development and assessment to determine their feasibility and potential impact.

3.5.4 Corporate taxation

Digital taxation as a source of EU budget revenue was initially proposed by the European Commission before the OECD agreed on Pillar One in October 2021 (Box 1). Some EU countries, including Austria, France, Italy and Spain, have introduced domestic digital service taxes (DSTs), while others have refrained from doing so domestically and have called for an EU-wide DST. However, opposition from some EU countries – fearing US trade retaliation – has prevented such a measure. Given shifts in US trade policy under President Trump, these concerns may now be more pressing.

An EU-wide DST would require unanimity, which remains highly unlikely. Countries with DSTs may also resent the opportunity cost of giving up the revenue to the EU. A more promising avenue could be to explore the feasibility of tariffs on digital services. Tariffs do not require unanimity and are more fit for a trade negotiation. If the US were to maintain across-the-board tariffs on EU goods, the EU should consider introducing tariffs on digital services, which could raise sizeable revenue.

Similarly, the EU could introduce new budget revenues to protect the single market from tax leakage and unfair tax competition. Domestic tax systems have historically been designed to avoid leakage. Tax jurisdiction extends to outbound revenue flows. For instance, a royalty, dividend or interest payment to another country will be subject to tax in the country where it arises – the source country. Service payments may also be subject to source taxation. Countries have historically reduced source taxation with selected partners in the context of tax treaties. Tax treaties are usually not concluded with countries with no or low taxation to avoid tax leakage. In other words, a comprehensive direct tax system includes 'external tax borders', which take the form of withholding taxes and anti-abuse provisions such as controlled foreign companies (CFC) mechanisms.

The EU has not yet established such external tax borders. Meanwhile, EU Court of Justice jurisprudence has resulted in the dismantling of internal borders within the EU, while some small open economies (such as Luxembourg and Ireland) designed their tax systems without preserving source taxation, even when outbound revenues flow to low- and no-tax jurisdictions. This offers external investors the possibility to channel income out of the EU with no or minimal taxation. This is particularly true for US tech companies and pharmaceutical companies (OECD, 2013).

The EU should seek to protect its own tax base by establishing external tax borders on flows of income leaving the EU. This should apply for corporate and personal income taxes, and potentially also wealth taxation. This would require tax treaty policy to be harmonised or, at least, the establishment of minimum rules that oblige countries to establish exit taxes for cases of high-net-worth individuals who leave with unrealised capital gains. Since this approach requires collective action and results in a collective benefit, it would justify an allocation of some of the collected revenues to the EU budget.

Even in the absence of common external tax borders, the implementation of the global minimum tax (Box 1) could have been an opportunity to allocate some revenues to the EU budget. Proceeds from the backstop Under-Taxed Profit Rule (UTPR, Box 1) could have been allocated to the EU budget, considering that there is a collective EU effort to ensure the proper implementation of the minimum tax for companies operating in the EU's single market. The UTPR in the EU is underpinned by a directive (Directive (EU) 2022/2523), which means it is already in the scope of EU competence, which is an additional justification for making proceeds available to the EU budget. We recommend that revenue generated by the implementation of the UTPR be allocated fully to the EU budget.

The UTPR would be applied to companies from countries that are not implementing the minimum tax. For the time being, this includes US and Chinese companies. On 20 January 2025, President Trump issued an executive order threatening countries that apply the UTPR to US companies with trade and tax retaliation[28]. While the number of

28 The White House, 'America First Trade Policy', 20 January 2025, https://www.whitehouse.gov/presidential-actions/2025/01/america-first-trade-policy/ The retaliatory measures have not at time of writing been spelled out, as bilateral negotiations between the US and various trading partners, including the EU, are still ongoing.

low-tax jurisdictions worldwide has fallen dramatically, as most have introduced the minimum tax through domestic top-up taxes, there remain offshore no- or low-tax jurisdictions, such as the Cayman Islands, where US companies could book their profits.

Another potential revenue source would be a single market levy on large companies operating in the EU. García Antón and Lejour (2023) calculated that a 0.11 percent levy on the turnover of firms with annual revenues exceeding €750 million could generate €10 billion per year. However, turnover taxes often lead to unintended distortions and are generally considered less fair than profit-based taxation (Aslam and Delgado Coelho, 2021).

3.5.5 Other revenue

In EU budget jargon, 'other revenue' refers to revenue sources outside the primary system of own resources. It includes taxes paid by EU staff on their salaries, interest on late payments, third-country contributions to EU programmes, administrative fees, fines and penalties, and proceeds from EU borrowing operations and investments. For example, in 2023, the United Kingdom contributed €8.8 billion to the EU budget in the context of the Brexit financial settlement, classified as 'other revenue'. This was more than the €7.2 billion raised by the non-recycled plastic levy, which is classified as an own resource.

Kubeková *et al* (2024) explored various strategies to boost these other resources within the EU's financial framework. These could include increasing the use of common debt, identifying further implementation user fees and including further third countries in specific EU programmes (eg Horizon Europe, thereby obtaining more contributions from such countries). However, Kubeková *et al* (2024) also acknowledged that the overall potential of other revenue remains limited because of legal constraints and the inherent volatility of such income sources.

Article 311 TFEU states that "*Without prejudice to other revenue, the budget shall be financed wholly from own resources*". Grund and

Steinbach (2023) argued that the ORD could classify 'other revenues' as own resources. This would require the unanimous agreement of EU members.

Even EU borrowing could be reclassified as an own resource by the ORD and used to finance regular EU budget expenditures, provided that a maximum amount is established and that debt servicing in any given year is secured by non-borrowed own resources, ie higher contributions from EU countries. This would enable the establishment of a permanent EU borrowing capacity, with the possibility of rolling over EU debt.

3.5.6 A proposal for a new revenue resource: the defence spending shortfall levy

We propose a new EU revenue source, linked to defence underspending by EU countries. This would reflect the growing importance of peace and security as European public goods, and the risk that some EU countries free-ride on the defence efforts of others.

Peace and security are vital for all of Europe, but are ensured through national defence and military spending. In 2023, defence spending ranged from just 0.2 percent of GDP in Ireland to 3.1 percent in Latvia (Figure 4). This variance creates a free-rider problem: countries spending less effectively benefit from those spending more.

Figure 4: General government defence spending/GDP, 2019 and 2023

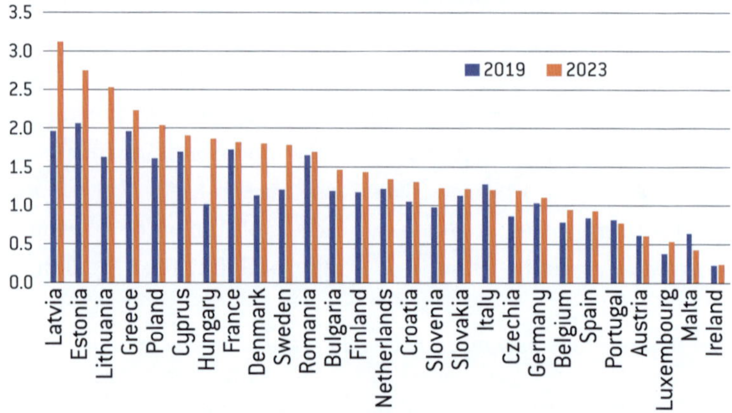

Source: Bruegel based on Eurostat's General government expenditure by function (COFOG) [gov_10a_exp] and Gross domestic product (GDP) and main components (output, expenditure and income) [nama_10_gdp] datasets. Note: countries are ordered according to defence spending/GDP in 2023.

A new EU budget resource would address this imbalance in national defence spending and incentivise low-spenders to spend more. The levy could be calculated on the basis of national underspending in defence, using one or more commonly agreed indicators. A straightforward option would be national defence spending as a share of GDP compared to a threshold, such as the EU average or a fixed value (eg 2 percent or 3 percent of GDP). Countries spending more would not contribute; only those spending less would. The levy could be recalculated annually to reflect changes in defence spending, which is currently rising rapidly in many EU member states. Given that defence capacity is largely shaped by historical investment, the levy could also be based on average defence spending over a longer period, such as the past two decades.

Like the plastic waste levy, which encourages recycling and has an environmental benefit, the defence levy would support an EU policy objective – in this case, stronger defence. In essence, it would function as a behavioural tax on governments, similar to the plastic waste levy or some of the climate-related levies discussed in section 3.5.2. It would also help address the free-rider problem by requiring countries that spend relatively little on defence to contribute more to the EU budget. The selected call rate – the percentage applied to the shortfall from the benchmark – would determine both the strength of the incentive for low-spending countries to increase their defence budgets, and the extent to which the levy redistributes the financial burden of the EU budget from high-spending to low-spending countries.

The European public good character of peace and security would justify channelling revenues related to defence underspending to the EU budget[29].

As an illustration, if the threshold was set at the EU average and the call rate at 25 percent, the 13 countries spending less than the EU average on defence in 2023 would contribute €8 billion annually to the EU budget. If the threshold was 2 percent of GDP with the same call rate, the 21 countries spending less than 2 percent of GDP on defence in 2023 would contribute about €30 billion per year (Table 7). The net impact of the levy on each country's contribution to the EU budget would depend on the amount paid under the levy minus the reduction in their GNI-based contributions resulting from the introduction of this levy. Table 7 also shows that applying the 2 percent threshold would reduce the EU budget contributions of 14 countries (those with higher-than-average defence spending/GDP shares), while increasing contributions for the remaining 13 countries.

If a fixed threshold were applied, contributions would in principle cease once a specific defence spending value is reached (eg 2 percent or 3 percent of GDP), while a levy based on deviation from the EU average would continue to generate revenue indefinitely, as it is highly unlikely that all countries will spend exactly the same amount on defence and thus

29 The EU budget could allocate more funds to certain defence industrial policy programmes, which are not prohibited by the EU Treaty. However, such decisions should be guided by the strategic value and desirability of increased EU spending in this area, and not by the potential introduction of a defence spending shortfall levy.

align precisely with the average.

The threshold spending rate should not be interpreted as a uniform target for all countries. Optimal defence spending levels vary by country and depend on a range of factors, including geographic location. Rather, the threshold rate should be viewed as an indicator discriminating between low and high defence spenders.

A complementary indicator could address defence procurement bias, penalising countries that unjustly favour domestic suppliers over suppliers from other EU countries (beyond an agreed threshold), thus hindering the development of a European defence single market. This would incentivise cross-border procurement and strengthen defence integration.

The legal basis for the proposed levy would be Article 311 TFEU, which underpins the ORD. Like the non-recycled plastic waste levy, or the corporate-tax based revenue proposal (section 3.4), no actual tax would be imposed. Instead, the levy would be calculated using statistical indicators, determining the size of each member state's contribution to the EU budget.

While politically sensitive, this new resource would underscore the EU's commitment to collective security. It would also give EU countries an incentive to align with the common strategic objective of increasing EU defence capabilities, while partially distributing the costs of European defence spending to those countries that spend relatively little.

Table 7: Impact of a defence spending shortfall levy on annual EU budget contributions using 2023 data, if the threshold was set at 2% of GDP and the call rate was 25%

	Defence spending in 2023 (% GDP)	Underspending relative to a 2% of GDP threshold (% GDP)	EU budget contribution by the new levy if the call rate was 25% (€ billions)	EU budget contribution if the same amount was distributed by GNI (€ billions)	Impact of the levy on contributions to the EU budget (€ billions	Impact of the levy on contributions to the EU budget (% GDP)
Latvia	3.12	0	0	0.066	-0.066	-0.17
Estonia	2.75	0	0	0.064	-0.064	-0.17
Lithuania	2.53	0	0	0.123	-0.123	-0.17
Greece	2.24	0	0	0.376	-0.376	-0.17
Poland	2.04	0	0	1.243	-1.243	-0.17
Cyprus	1.91	0.09	0.007	0.049	-0.042	-0.13
Hungary	1.87	0.13	0.066	0.331	-0.265	-0.13
France	1.82	0.18	1.238	4.961	-3.723	-0.13
Denmark	1.81	0.19	0.181	0.668	-0.487	-0.13
Sweden	1.79	0.21	0.284	0.974	-0.690	-0.13
Romania	1.70	0.30	0.244	0.544	-0.299	-0.09
Bulgaria	1.47	0.53	0.127	0.155	-0.029	-0.03
Finland	1.44	0.56	0.382	0.473	-0.090	-0.03
Netherlands	1.34	0.66	1.749	1.827	-0.077	-0.01

	Defence spending in 2023 (% GDP)	Underspending relative to a 2% of GDP threshold (% GDP)	EU budget contribution by the new levy if the call rate was 25% (€ billions)	EU budget contribution if the same amount was distributed by GNI (€ billions)	Impact of the levy on contributions to the EU budget (€ billions	Impact of the levy on contributions to the EU budget (% GDP)
Croatia	1.31	0.69	0.134	0.134	0.001	0.00
Slovenia	1.23	0.77	0.123	0.109	0.014	0.02
Slovakia	1.21	0.79	0.243	0.209	0.034	0.03
Italy	1.20	0.80	4.257	3.658	0.599	0.03
Czechia	1.20	0.80	0.637	0.540	0.097	0.03
Germany	1.11	0.89	9.336	7.475	1.861	0.04
Belgium	0.95	1.05	1.570	1.043	0.527	0.09
Spain	0.93	1.07	3.995	2.573	1.422	0.09
Portugal	0.77	1.23	0.823	0.450	0.373	0.14
Austria	0.61	1.39	1.646	0.817	0.829	0.18
Luxembourg	0.54	1.46	0.295	0.097	0.198	0.24
Malta	0.43	1.57	0.081	0.031	0.050	0.24
Ireland	0.24	1.76	2.239	0.670	1.569	0.31
Sum			29.659	29.659	0.000	

Source: Bruegel based on Eurostat's General government expenditure by function (COFOG) [gov_10a_exp] and Gross domestic product (GDP) and main components (output, expenditure and income) [nama_10_gdp] datasets. Note: countries are ordered according to defence spending/GDP in 2023.

3.6 Revenue correction mechanisms

The Fontainebleau European Summit in June 1984 established the principle that "*any Member State sustaining a budgetary burden which is excessive in relation to its relative prosperity may benefit from a correction at the appropriate time*". The summit introduced a correction to the UK's contribution (the 'UK rebate') and a reduction in Germany's contribution to the UK rebate (the 'rebate on the rebate'). These precedents led to the creation of several other correction mechanisms, benefiting Austria, Denmark, Germany, the Netherlands and Sweden (Darvas, 2019b).

Denmark and Ireland (and the UK while still an EU member) also benefitted from corrections related to their non-participation in specific security and citizenship policies, for which these countries have (or had) Treaty-based opt-outs.

The EU budget's rebate system has become increasingly complex, non-transparent and unjustified[30]. The five countries benefiting the most from rebates - Austria, Denmark, Germany, the Netherlands and Sweden - contribute less to the EU budget as shares of their GNI than most other member states, particularly those with lower GNI *per capita* (Figure 5). The Fontainebleau principle does not apply to the five rich countries that benefit from rebates.

30 The Danish and Irish corrections related to opt-outs from security and citizenship policies do have a justification.

Figure 5: GNI per capita vs national contributions to the EU budget, 2021-2023

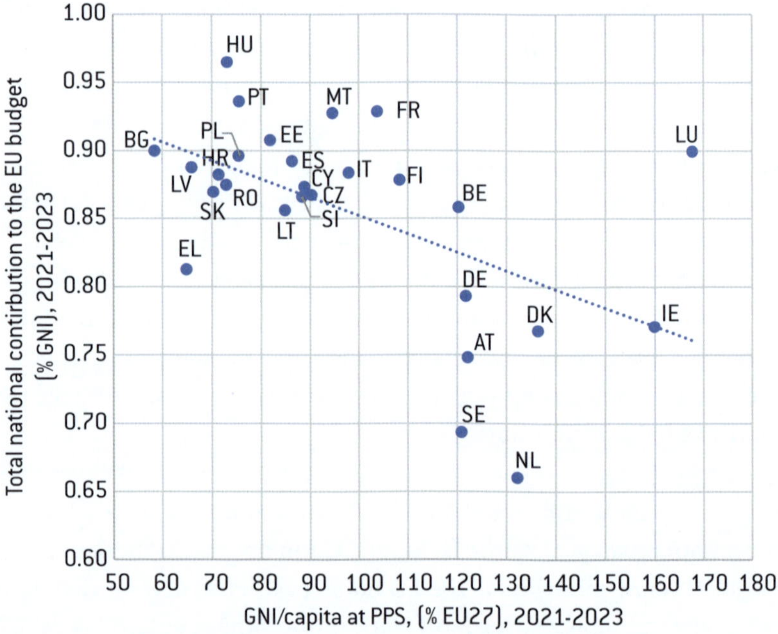

Source: Bruegel based on budget execution data from the European Commission and the November 2024 AMECO dataset. Note: total national contributions are composed of GNI-based own resources, VAT-based own resources, non-recycled plastic packaging waste own resources, and the various reductions and adjustments. PPS = purchasing power standards. The dotted line shows the linear regression fit.

The European Court of Auditors (ECA, 2005, 2006, 2012) has long criticised the EU budget's rebate system for various shortcomings. These include the absence of clear criteria to assess objectively whether a budgetary burden is excessive and when an EU country qualifies for a correction; the lack of a monitoring mechanism to determine whether an EU country benefitting from a correction still qualifies for it; and the absence of a mechanism to evaluate whether other EU countries that do not receive corrections might now qualify. These criticisms remain valid.

There would be no justification for rebates if the EU budget were devoted exclusively to providing European public goods. However, as demonstrated in chapter 2, a significant portion of EU spending does not align with the concept of EPGs. The optimal solution would be to reform EU budget expenditure to focus solely on the provision of EPGs and to eliminate rebates entirely. If such a reform proves politically unfeasible, then at minimum, the justification for rebates should be articulated clearly, and the current *ad-hoc*, opaque, complex, and regressive rebate system should be replaced with a transparent correction mechanism based on well-defined principles.

3.7 Conclusions

A shift away from the dominance of GNI-based own resources towards revenue sources more closely aligned with EU competences, along with a higher share of EPG spending, could help redirect the focus in EU budget discussions away from the net-balances debate. It would also better support the achievement of the EU's objectives. However, any increase in the EU budget will bring with it an opportunity cost for national budgets. Moreover, if the cross-country distribution of new revenue resources differs from that of GNI, it will alter the cross-country distribution of contributions to the EU budget. The difficulties in advancing European Commission EU budget revenue proposals indicate that the political appetite for introducing new EU budget revenues is limited.

In light of the analysis throughout this chapter, we believe that a more ambitious and strategic approach is needed to diversify EU budget revenues. While recognising the political constraints, we support a balanced portfolio of new own resources that conform with the principles of Treaty alignment, fairness, policy coherence and revenue stability.

First, revenues linked to the ETS and CBAM – as proposed by the Commission – stand out as legitimate genuine own resources. They are rooted in EU-level policies with clear environmental objectives and Treaty-based competence. Despite their declining revenue potential over the long term, they would provide stable revenues during the next

MFF. We support allocating a greater share of these revenues to the EU budget by raising the proposed 75 percent ceiling for CBAM (section 3.3.4) and expanding the product coverage in future Commission proposals. Among current revenues, we recommend allocating the full amount of customs duty revenues to the EU budget, except for a small collection cost.

Second, we recommend the establishment of external tax borders for flows of corporate and personal income leaving the EU, and potentially also for departing wealth. This would require tax treaty policy to be harmonised or, at least, the establishment of minimum rules obliging countries to apply exit taxes to high-net-worth individuals leaving an EU country with unrealised capital gains.

Third, we see strong merit in considering a dedicated EU budget revenue stream derived from the Under Taxed Profit Rule (UTPR) under Pillar Two of the OECD/G20 global tax agreement. The UTPR represents a collective European effort to enforce fair minimum taxation for multinational enterprises and to protect the single market from tax avoidance by foreign firms. Because the EU has implemented the UTPR through a directive and applies it in a coordinated manner, there is a compelling case to allocate its proceeds (or a large share of them) to the EU budget.

Fourth, there is an opportunity to introduce EU-level climate-related levies in hard-to-abate sectors, especially aviation and shipping. These sectors are currently under-taxed, responsible for a significant share of emissions and difficult to regulate through national policies alone. A kerosene tax, a harmonised ticket levy and/or an expanded ETS covering international aviation and maritime routes could yield new revenue streams, while aligning with the EU's climate goals. Agriculture also contributes significantly to harmful emissions and environmental degradation, yet it remains largely exempt from emissions and environmental taxation. Including this sector in the ETS or applying related taxes would support the EU's climate and environmental objectives. We therefore support the development of such sector-specific climate taxes as EU budget resources.

Beyond these more conventional proposals, we also see merit in exploring a defence-related own resource as a forward-looking and politically resonant innovation. While politically sensitive, such a resource would underscore the EU's commitment to collective security. Even if the EU budget cannot finance defence and military expenditures, the EPG character of security would justify channelling such a revenue source to the MFF. Alternatively, the revenue could be channelled to a non-MFF fund that would finance common defence projects in which all 27 EU countries participate. As such, a defence spending shortfall levy (section 3.5) warrants further conceptual and political development.

In the absence of a comprehensive reform of the EU's own resources, GNI-based contributions will continue to dominate EU budget revenues. Consequently, any new spending on EPGs and NGEU debt service will need to rely on this source. For servicing NGEU-related liabilities, EU countries, in the 2020 ORD, committed 0.6 percent of their GNIs annually until 2058. This amount is almost ten times more than what will be needed.

The EU budget's rebate system has become complex and opaque and is no longer justified. It also makes national contributions to the EU budget regressive, because countries with higher GNI *per capita* tend to contribute smaller shares of their GNIs to the EU budget. This is inconsistent with Protocol No. 28 TFEU. The optimal solution is to focus EU spending exclusively on EPGs and eliminate all rebates. If this is not politically feasible, the rationale for rebates should be clearly stated and the current opaque system replaced with a transparent, rules-based correction mechanism.

4 Lessons from the EU's current spending instruments

4.1 Context

The EU budget has long been criticised, including by Draghi (2024), who argued that its effectiveness is hindered by fragmentation, complexity and rigidity. He recommended refocusing, simplifying and streamlining EU funding, including by regrouping and significantly reducing the number of funding programmes, and by harmonising rules and requirements across programmes.

Some of these ideas were reflected in the roadmap for the next Multiannual Financial Framework (MFF) proposed by European Commission (2025b), which envisages three main spending pillars (not including European public administration):

1. A large share of current EU budget spending, including agricultural and cohesion policies, would be merged into a yet-to-be-named mega-fund. This fund would be accessed via the implementation by each EU country of a national *"plan with key reforms and investments"* using a performance-based framework;
2. A European Competitiveness Fund would create investment capacity for strategic sectors and critical technologies, and would include the current Horizon Europe research funding instruments;
3. A new external action fund would integrate the EU programmes outside the Union.

The Commission would manage the second and third pillars directly, reflecting common EU industrial policy, foreign and partnerships policies. As outlined in chapter 2, we believe that some European Competitiveness Fund spending, such as on research and de-risking of investment, should be allocated to EU level because of its European public good (EPG) character. The new external action fund should be treated similarly. Public goods delivered under these funds fall under our 'full EPG' classification, with all governance aspects carried out by the EU. In the context of additional spending needs, as identified in chapter 2, international climate finance would fall under the external action fund, fully funded and delivered by the EU.

In contrast, the first pillar, including cohesion policy and the Common Agricultural Policy, would give EU members more discretion over spending the funds. Decentralised implementation of such spending can have advantages because EU members are likely to have better information on the potential value-added of specific projects, and have greater (combined) administrative capacity than the EU. We classify EPGs under this fund as nationally delivered, as outlined in chapter 2. For example, financing for environmental initiatives should happen at an EU level, while delivery is better carried out at national level as it requires information on local circumstances and needs. However, decentralised implementation can also lead to increased funding of national public goods rather than EPGs, or spending that does not align with EU goals. Performance-based budgeting can be a powerful instrument to deal with these issues and ensure the enforcement of EU-level rules and objectives.

Therefore, the Commission's intention to apply a performance framework for pillar one and directly manage pillars two and three is welcome. However, the current proposal lacks space for 'full EPGs', such as cross-border infrastructure, that do not align with the objectives of the Competitiveness Fund. There are two options for including such EPGs in the next MFF. First, they could be included under pillar 1 by requiring a minimum threshold for cross-border projects in national plans. Second, a fourth pillar could be added, which would cover EPGs that should fall fully under EU-level governance, while not qualifying for inclusion in the Competitiveness Fund or the external action fund.

The proposed national reform and investment plans under the first pillar resemble the National Recovery and Resilience Plans (NRRPs) prepared by EU countries in 2021 and 2022 to access the Recovery and Resilience Facility (RRF), the largest funding component of NextGenerationEU (NGEU), the EU's flagship pandemic recovery and structural transformation instrument[31]. The RRF's mid-term review assessed it as a great success (European Commission, 2025a), except for a higher-than-expected administrative burden. The Commission believes that this problem can be mitigated. This chapter argues that while the RRF was an important and useful instrument to signal the EU's determination to address a common shock with a common fiscal instrument, it faced some design issues, and offers important lessons for the first pillar of the next MFF. Current performance-based instruments within the MFF for cohesion policy and CAP also offer useful lessons, which we also analyse in this chapter.

4.2 Lessons from the RRF

There has been a long-standing effort to make the EU budget more performance-oriented. Milestones in this include the European Commission's 2010 budget review, the 2015 EU Budget Focused on Results initiative (European Commission, 2017) and the 2018 revision of the EU budget financial regulation, which introduced requirements for *ex-ante* definition of programme objectives and performance monitoring.

Kristalina Georgieva, then Vice-President of the European Commission, noted in 2015: *"we can build a road with 0 percent error rate but if it goes nowhere, it is still a road to nowhere, and it is a 100 percent waste of our taxpayers' money"* (European Commission, 2017). In other words, completing a project and measuring its success based on output indicators (eg a road built) does not ensure that the project

31 See 'Recovery and Resilience Facility', European Commission, https://commission.europa.eu/business-economy-euro/economic-recovery/recovery-and-resilience-facility_en.

has delivered results that benefit society.

4.2.1 Performance-based budgeting

Public funding that is contingent on measurable results, rather than merely on expenditures incurred, is commonly referred to as performance-based funding (OECD, 2007). Performance-based budgeting involves *"the systemic use of information about outputs, results and/or impacts to inform, influence and/or determine the allocation of public funds,"* according to the European Court of Auditors (ECA, 2021).

To enable such an approach, four categories of indicators are typically distinguished:

1. Input: the financial, human, material, administrative or regulatory means used to implement a project or programme.
2. Output: something produced or achieved by a project, such as the delivery of a training course or the construction of a road.
3. Result: the immediate effect of a project or programme on its completion, such as the improved employability of course participants, or easier mobility following the construction of a new road.
4. Impact: the broader, long-term consequences of a project or programme, such as socio-economic gains for the wider population.

Box 3 gives examples of the first three types of indicator, taken from selected NRRPs. NRRPs were evaluated by the Commission and approved by the Council[32]. Impact indicators, which are generally observable only over a longer period, were rightly not included in the NRRPs.

32 NRRPs and related assessments can be found at https://commission.europa.eu/business-economy-euro/economic-recovery/recovery-and-resilience-facility/country-pages_en.

Box 3: NRRP performance indicator examples

Input:

- Number of projects for which a grant agreement has been signed for remediation of wasteland or urbanised areas: 90 by 2022Q1 and 200 by 2023Q1 (France);
- Enterprises receiving support for investment in innovation in the circular economy and bio-economy: at least 10,000 by 2024Q4 and 15,000 by 2026Q2 (Italy);
- Funding provided to small and medium-sized enterprises (SMEs) in the Agents of Change Programme: 100 percent of the budget of €300 million by 2023Q4, supporting at least 15,000 SMEs in digital transformation (Spain).

Output:

- Completion or continuation of 100 consultations with funding programme beneficiaries, which may also be part of a more encompassing investment advisory service, by 2024Q3 (Germany);
- At least two static monitoring stations and at least 10 mobile monitoring stations in the North Sea, installed and operational by 2026Q1 (the Netherlands);
- Creation of at least 50 centres of excellence and innovation in vocational training by 2024Q4 (Spain).

Result:

- Greenhouse gas emissions avoided compared to the 'before-investment' situation: 3.5 million tonnes of carbon dioxide equivalent (MtCO2eq) by 2021Q2 and 5 MtCO2eq by 2022Q4 (France);
- Variation between the average three best-performing regions and the three worst-performing regions in separate waste collection rates reduced by 20 percentage points by 2024Q4 (Italy);
- Number of people killed or seriously injured as a result of road accidents in urban municipalities compared to the reference year 2019 reduced by 25 percent by 2026Q1 (Romania).

Source: Darvas and Welslau (2023).

Performance-based budgeting, as defined by the European Court of Auditors, can be justified as a solution to two types of moral hazard problems (Darvas *et al*, 2023).

First, making fund disbursement conditional on project outputs, rather than costs, addresses moral hazard in project implementation. If funding simply reimburses expenses, there is little incentive for cost efficiency. Linking funding to outputs (eg completion of a tunnel) encourages projects to be delivered cost-effectively. Similarly, making fund disbursements conditional on physical inputs expected *ex ante* rather than incurred costs, allows for partial disbursement during implementation while maintaining cost discipline.

Second, using indicators of results (and possibly impact) helps mitigate moral hazard in project selection. Applicants usually have private information about the likely social value of their projects. By focusing on results, performance-based funding reduces the risk that 'roads to nowhere' will be financed. As Moynihan and Beazley (2016) put it: *"All performance budgeting efforts have a common goal—to focus the mindset and behavior of public officials on policy priorities and results."*

A common concern is that impact indicators expose project implementers to excessive risk, as even well-executed projects may underperform because of external shocks (eg the global financial crisis or the COVID-19 pandemic). However, this risk does not apply to result indicators as defined by the European Court of Auditors, which measure the immediate usability of project outputs rather than their broader socio-economic impacts.

4.2.2 The Recovery and Resilience Facility is not performance-based

The RRF marked a notable shift in EU budgeting methods. Unlike traditional cost reimbursement, RRF funds are disbursed based on achieving milestones and targets, as set out in NRRPs.

Although the preamble of the RRF Regulation (Regulation (EU) 2021/241) references *"the performance-based nature of the Facility"*, neither the Regulation nor the Commission's implementation guidance require reporting on actual results. The preamble states that *"for reasons of efficiency and simplification in the financial management of the Facility, Union financial support for recovery and resilience plans should take the form of financing based on the achievement of results measured by reference to milestones and targets indicated in the approved recovery and resilience plans."*

However, Article (2) of the regulation defines milestones and targets as *"measures of progress towards the achievement of a reform or an investment"*. The expression *"measures of progress towards"* suggests a focus on processes rather than true results, as the European Court of Auditors and OECD definitions would require.

Moreover, the Commission's guidance for preparing NRRPs encouraged the use of input and output indicators while discouraging the use of result and impact indicators. According to the Commission's guidance (European Commission, 2021):

> *"Milestones and targets should be clear and realistic, and the proposed indicators relevant, acceptable and robust. They can reflect different stages of the implementation of reforms and investments, either based on input indicators (e.g. resources provided, which can be financial, human, administrative) or preferably output indicators (e.g. number of workers trained, numbers of renovated schools).*
>
> *"Overall, it is important that milestones and targets remain within the control of the Member State and are not conditional on external factors such as the macroeconomic outlook or the evolution of the labour market. Impact indicators (e.g. decrease in the number of unfilled vacancies in the IT sector) should be avoided given the unpredictability of such indicators and their dependence on other factors outside the control of the Member State."*

While the concern about external risks is valid, this guidance raises two issues. First, it fails to distinguish between broader impact indicators and more immediate result indicators and thus discourages the use of the latter. Second, the example used (*"decrease in the number of unfilled vacancies in the IT sector"*) would actually qualify as a result indicator under the European Court of Auditors definition. If a training programme is well targeted based on identified labour market needs, then using such a result indicator would be appropriate. It would in principle address the moral-hazard problem related to project selection (section 4.2.1) and would expose the country to minimal risk outside its control.

Box 3 and the online annex of Darvas *et al* (2023) demonstrate that several EU countries could design meaningful result indicators without exposing themselves to excessive external risk. However, possibly because of the Commission's discouragement of result indicators, the numbers of such indicators varied significantly across countries (Table 8). France, Germany and the Netherlands included in their NRRPs very few result indicators, in absolute numbers or as a share of total indicators. By contrast, Finland, Italy and Romania included many more result indicators, both in number and proportion. Spain falls between the two groups. Therefore, the French, German and Dutch plans align more with the process-focused definition of milestones in the RRF Regulation, while the Finnish, Italian and Romanian plans show a clearer results orientation[33].

33 The low number of result indicators in the French and German plans cannot be attributed to limited access to RRF funding. France (€37 billion in grants) and Germany (€28 billion in grants) obtained more funding than Finland (€1.8 billion) and Romania (€12 billion in grants and €15 billion in loans), yet Finland and Romania included many more result indicators and fewer input indicators, both in absolute terms and as shares of total targets.

Table 8: Classification of NRRP target indicators, selected EU countries

	Finland	France	Germany	Italy	Netherlands	Romania	Spain
				Number of targets			
Input	11	51	41	62	20	25	67
Output	38	51	29	191	31	190	107
Result	10	3	5	59	3	39	20
All	59	105	75	312	54	254	194
				Percent of all targets			
Input	19	49	55	20	37	10	35
Output	64	49	39	61	57	75	55
Result	17	3	7	19	6	15	10
All	100	100	100	100	100	100	100

Source: Bruegel based on Darvas *et al* (2023).

One potential justification for relying mainly on input and output indicators could be the Commission's direct involvement in negotiating national recovery plans, which may have mitigated moral hazard in project selection. However, this involvement is unlikely to have fully eliminated the risk: the Commission had to negotiate 27 complex NRRPs within tight deadlines, making thorough evaluation of each project improbable. Incorporating more result indicators could have provided an additional safeguard, ensuring greater alignment with social value objectives.

Moreover, the Commission's role in managing the RRF (negotiating the NRRPs, evaluating and proposing their approval to the Council and publicly reporting on RRF successes) has expanded significantly. The Commission's evaluation of NRRPs cannot be considered fully objective (section 4.2.3). More use of result indicators would help address concerns about transparency, political interference and unequal treatment, and would reinforce the credibility of the Commission's evaluations.

The RRF's focus on processes rather than results appears inconsistent with the EU's frequent advocacy in favour of results-based approaches. Explicitly focusing on the social value added by funded projects could help meet public expectations of a genuine performance-based instrument. More use of result indicators would also counter criticism about the capacities of EU countries in selecting appropriate projects and the EU's ability to monitor them effectively, thereby enhancing public trust in EU spending.

Finally, the Commission has also noted that the current RRF framework does not foresee the tracking of actual expenditure (ie *ex-post* assessments), noting that constant monitoring of milestones and targets suffices to evaluate performance[34]. This is inherently at odds with the idea of results-based performance budgeting, which can only fulfil its full potential in an *ex-post* evaluation.

The RRF marked a turning point in EU fiscal governance. It introduced a novel model of financing, disbursing funds based on the achievement of predefined milestones and targets, rather than through traditional cost reimbursement. This approach provided the EU with a unique opportunity to move towards a more performance-oriented budgetary model, one that prioritises the realisation of strategic objectives. However, our analysis shows that the RRF has fallen short of delivering accurate performance-based budgeting. Most notably, the RRF framework relies heavily on input and output indicators and often avoids result indicators. In practice, many milestones and targets were too focused on processes rather than outcomes, weakening the facility's potential impacts[35].

4.2.3 The increased role of the European Commission cuts both ways

The RRF framework significantly expanded the European Commission's role, with both benefits and drawbacks. The Commission helped countries prepare their NRRPs, support that was or should have been

34 See replies of the European Commission to ECA (2023), available at https://www.eca.europa.eu/Lists/ECAReplies/COM-Replies-SR-2023-26/COM-Replies-SR-2023-26_EN.pdf.

35 ECA (2025) also concluded that the RRF is not a performance-based instrument.

highly beneficial. Thanks to its skilled experts and deep country-specific knowledge, the Commission likely improved the quality of the NRRPs from the early stages. The Commission can also factor in the broader European perspective and encourage countries to do this as well.

However, the bilateral nature of the Commission-member states' discussions limited transparency. The long length and differing structures and indicators in NRRPs made cross-country scrutiny difficult. Some plans exceeded 1,000 pages, and milestones and targets varied widely. While adaptation to national circumstances is essential, this variation made the plans difficult to compare. Common indicators cover only a subset of RRF activities and focus primarily on inputs and outputs, not results. The Commission did not assess the ambition levels of plans, raising concerns about uneven value for European money across countries.

Moreover, the Commission's strong interest in portraying the RRF as a success may have made assessments less objective, both during initial evaluations and when the mid-term review of the RRF was done. Two issues in particular suggest that evaluations may not have been fully objective: 1) the initial assessments of the recovery plans (section 4.2.3.1), and 2) the mid-term review's assessment of progress on European Semester country-specific recommendations (section 4.2.3.2).

4.2.3.1 Concerns about the objectivity of initial plan evaluations

The Commission assessed NRRPs against 11 criteria defined in Annex 5 of the RRF Regulation, using a three-tier scale: A (criterion largely met), B (moderately met) and C (met to a limited extent). Assessments were strikingly uniform: virtually all plans were graded A for most criteria and B for cost justification, with only minor exceptions in three cases (Table 9). Plans that were submitted later, including that of the Netherlands (often considered to have a high-quality budgeting process), received identical grades, including a B for cost justification.

Darvas (2022) questioned the objectivity of this uniform grading. For instance, the Commission's evaluation of Italy's NRRP listed numerous cost justification issues, while for Austria, a single sentence sufficed to justify the B grade - by referring to parts of the plan in which funding criteria and beneficiaries were not yet sufficiently known. Similar inconsistencies appeared in the detailed assessments of other countries' plans. Furthermore, it is implausible that none of the 27 governments could fully justify costs, especially given the expertise available in national finance ministries and development banks. The hypothesis that the Commission deliberately assigned a uniform B grade for cost justification for all countries, and almost uniform A grades for the other criteria, cannot be excluded. If this hypothesis is correct, how can the assessments be trusted? And what guarantee is there that the Commission's assessment of the national plans to be prepared for the first pillar of the 2028-2034 MFF will be more objective?

Table 9: The Commission's evaluation of NRRPs

	(1) Comprehensive and balanced response	(2) Country-specific recommendations	(3) Growth, jobs, economic, social and institutional resilience	(4) Do no significant harm to environment	(5) Green transition	(6) Digital transition	(7) Lasting impact	(8) Monitoring and implementation	(9) Cost justification	(10) Preventing corruption, fraud and conflicts of interest	(11) Coherence
Austria	A	A	A	A	A	A	A	A	B	A	A
Belgium	A	A	A	A	A	A	A	A	B	A	B
Bulgaria	A	A	A	A	A	A	A	A	B	A	A
Croatia	A	A	A	A	A	A	A	A	B	A	A
Cyprus	A	A	A	A	A	A	A	A	B	A	A
Czechia	A	A	A	A	A	A	A	B	B	A	B
Denmark	A	A	A	A	A	A	A	A	B	A	A
Estonia	A	A	A	A	A	A	A	A	B	A	B
Finland	A	A	A	A	A	A	A	A	B	A	A
France	A	A	A	A	A	A	A	A	B	A	A
Germany	A	A	A	A	A	A	A	A	B	A	A
Greece	A	A	A	A	A	A	A	A	B	A	A
Hungary	A	A	A	A	A	A	A	A	B	A	A
Italy	A	A	A	A	A	A	A	A	B	A	A
Ireland	A	A	A	A	A	A	A	A	B	A	A
Lativa	A	A	A	A	A	A	A	A	B	A	A
Lithuania	A	A	A	A	A	A	A	A	B	A	A
Luxembourg	A	A	A	A	A	A	A	A	B	A	A
Malta	A	A	A	A	A	A	A	A	B	A	A
Netherlands	A	A	A	A	A	A	A	A	B	A	A
Poland	A	A	A	A	A	A	A	A	B	A	A
Portugal	A	A	A	A	A	A	A	A	B	A	A
Romania	A	A	A	A	A	A	A	A	B	A	A
Slovakia	A	A	A	A	A	A	A	A	B	A	A
Slovenia	A	A	A	A	A	A	A	A	B	A	A
Spain	A	A	A	A	A	A	A	A	B	A	A
Sweden	A	A	A	A	A	A	A	A	B	A	A

Source: Bruegel. Note: nine criteria are assessed on a scale of A, B or C. A: criterion is met to a large extent; B: criterion is met to a moderate or medium extent: and C: criterion is met to a limited extent. The 'do no significant harm' (criterion 4) and 'preventing corruption, fraud and

4.2.3.2 Implementation of European Semester recommendations is less impressive than claimed

The RRF Regulation required NRRPs to address *"all or a significant subset"* of the country-specific recommendations (CSRs) made during the European Semester[36], the process of coordination of economic, budgetary, employment and social policies within the EU, intended to ensure that national policies align with EU rules and objectives. Within this framework, the Commission proposes CSRs for each EU country, which are approved, after possible amendments, by the Council, usually in July each year. To assess whether NRRPs properly incorporated CSRs, the Commission evaluated compliance with the 2019 and 2020 CSRs for most countries, while for the Netherlands and Hungary, the 2019, 2020 and 2022 CSRs were the benchmarks.

According to the Commission's mid-term review (European Commission, 2025), EU countries made *"significant progress"* in addressing CSRs. However, data shows that implementation rates for the 2019-2020 CSRs changed little compared to earlier years, except for fiscal recommendations (Figure 6).

Implementation of fiscal recommendations remained high in 2021-2024. However, this increase mainly reflected fiscal recommendations that were easy to meet because they aligned with what governments were doing already: providing fiscal support during the pandemic and using RRF funds. These recommendations were similar for all EU countries and required little country-specific action[37].

Meanwhile, CSR implementation in more challenging areas, such as labour-market reform, governance and taxation, remained close to or below pre-pandemic levels in 2022–2024 (Figure 6). The Commission's mid-term review failed to acknowledge that CSR implementation in these areas did not improve.

36 However, the interpretation of a *"significant subset"* is not defined in the RRF Regulation or by the Commission.

37 See Darvas (2024) for a textual comparison across countries of the 2020-2021 CSRs.

Figure 6: CSR implementation after one year (by policy area, all EU countries)

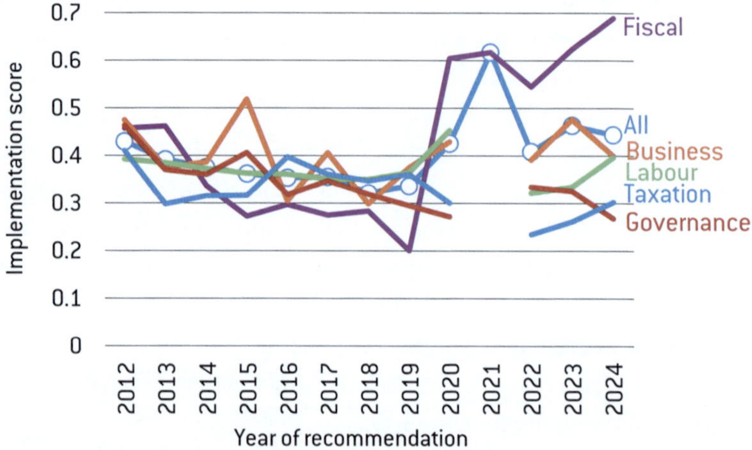

Source: Bruegel based on the European Commission's CSR database. Note: qualitative scores assigned by the Commission are converted to numerical scores, following Deroose and Griesse (2014): full implementation = 1; substantial progress = 0.75; some progress = 0.5; limited progress = 0.25; and no progress = 0. There were only fiscal recommendations in 2021.

To conclude, the implementation of the RRF exposed significant governance and transparency shortcomings. The European Commission played a far more important role than in the traditional MFF process: advising on national plans, evaluating them and proposing disbursements. While this helped improve plan quality, the bilateral and closed-door nature of negotiations limited transparency, while the different plan structures limited cross-country comparability. Moreover, the Commission's interest in showcasing the RRF's success may have made it hesitant to criticise underperformance, as indicated by uniform and overly positive initial plan assessments, and a mid-term review that overlooked weak reform delivery in critical policy areas.

4.2.4 If the RRF provided value for money cannot be properly assessed

The Commission's treatment all NRRPs as being of equally high quality, and the assumption that no government could fully justify costs, have implications in terms of evaluating the value of RRF funds. Because of the limited number of result indicators, it is not possible to form a comprehensive view on the outcomes achieved by the RRF. In addition, the milestones and targets varied widely across countries, making impossible cross-country comparisons, and therefore assessments of difficulty and value for money. As a result, the actual value for money achieved likely differs significantly between EU countries.

The pillar one flagship instrument under the next MFF (section 4.1) should be designed to address these shortcomings. Standardised indicators for performance assessment should be adopted and cross-country comparability enabled to ensure a clearer understanding of the value of EU-level spending.

Another concern with the RRF with implications for the next MFF is the very limited share of pan-European projects in NRRPs. Although the Commission encouraged the use of RRF funds to support cross-border initiatives that would deliver high European added value, most EU countries ultimately scaled back such ambitions in favour of national projects. If this national focus persists, a major risk in basing a large share of the next MFF on national plans will be the further marginalisation of pan-European initiatives, undermining the very goal of collective European action.

These problems are further compounded by budgetary control challenges. Begg *et al* (2025b) highlighted several issues, including vague definitions of milestones and targets, inconsistent compliance guidelines, shortcomings in data management (such as the need for manual data entry when national and EU systems are not integrated), overlapping audits and associated administrative burdens. Potential improvements include adopting a single-audit approach, streamlining the verification of milestones and targets and better aligning EU and national audit systems. Striking the right balance between accountability and flexibility – to allow for adjustments in response to unforeseen challenges while maintaining ambition – will be essential to refine the RRF model and design effective performance-based instruments under the next MFF.

4.2.5 The slower-than-planned absorption rate of RRF funds is not actually problematic

Another concern in relation to the effectiveness of the RRF is the pace of fund disbursement. The European Court of Auditors (ECA, 2024c) concluded that disbursements are progressing with delays, which could jeopardise the achievement of the RRF's objectives. Common challenges for EU countries include external shocks, underestimation of implementation timelines, limited administrative capacity and uncertainties related to RRF implementation rules (eg the 'do no significant harm' principle) (ECA, 2024c).

The European Commission has accepted many of the European Court of Auditors' recommendations. However, it has emphasised that the RRF is not solely designed to ensure full disbursement of funds, but rather to support the achievement of agreed objectives, since disbursements are conditional on milestones and targets. Therefore, the Commission rejected the European Court of Auditors' recommendation that it should *"mitigate the risk of funding non-completed measures"*[38].

Is slow absorption of the RRF funds truly problematic? Are such delays inherent to performance-based funding instruments, and does this imply that a future performance-based instrument under the next MFF would likely face similar delays? Our answer to these questions is no, for three main reasons:

1. Various shocks occurred during RRF implementation (inflation, war, energy crisis, decoupling from Russia); these have complicated implementation, often requiring time-consuming revisions to NRRPs.

38 See the replies of European Commission to ECA (2024), available at https://www.eca.europa.eu/Lists/ECAReplies/COM-Replies-SR-2024-13/COM-Replies-SR-2024-13_EN.pdf.

2. EU countries had to absorb unprecedented amounts of EU funds, often significantly exceeding cohesion allocations (Table 10). For example, Italy and Spain will in principle receive nearly twice as much in RRF grants as they do from cohesion policy, and even more in RRF loans than in RRF grants.
3. The feasibility of EU countries absorbing RRF funding in addition to all other MFF funding, including unspent funds from the 2014-2020 period, while implementing new cohesion funds under the 2021-2027 MFF, was already in doubt at the RRF's inception (Darvas, 2020)[39].

It is also notable that the absorption rate for RRF funds, measured as cumulative disbursement relative to the total available envelope, is higher than those for the three main cohesion funds (Figure 7). The difference likely lies in the incentive provided by the timeline: RRF funds must be absorbed by 2026, whereas cohesion funds may continue to be absorbed up to three years after the end of the seven-year MFF period. For instance, only 62 percent of 2007-2013 and 52 percent of 2014-2020 cohesion funds were absorbed by the end of their respective MFF periods, with the remainder absorbed subsequently.

The RRF Regulation prohibits disbursement beyond 2026, a restriction that merits reconsideration, because of the three main reasons for the slower-than-planned implementation, as summarised above. If RRF projects are valuable from a European perspective, as they are intended to be, then adhering to the 2026 deadline without even a short extension risks leaving important projects incomplete and may put governments under pressure to rush implementation, potentially undermining quality and effectiveness.

We thus conclude that the low absorption rate of RRF funds

39 Therefore, it is not surprising either that Cohesion Fund absorption in the first four years of the current MFF has been less than in the first four years of the previous two MFFs (Figure 7).

does not pose an issue for the RRF and does not mean that a similar performance-based instrument in the next MFF will also be subject to significant implementation delays. The RRF delays have arisen for specific reasons: unexpected development, the underestimated challenge of absorbing much larger amounts of EU funds than in the past and overly ambitious implementation plans. The design of future performance-based MFF instruments should learn lessons from these specific factors.

Figure 7: Absorption rate of cohesion and RRF funds (in % of funds available for the total period)

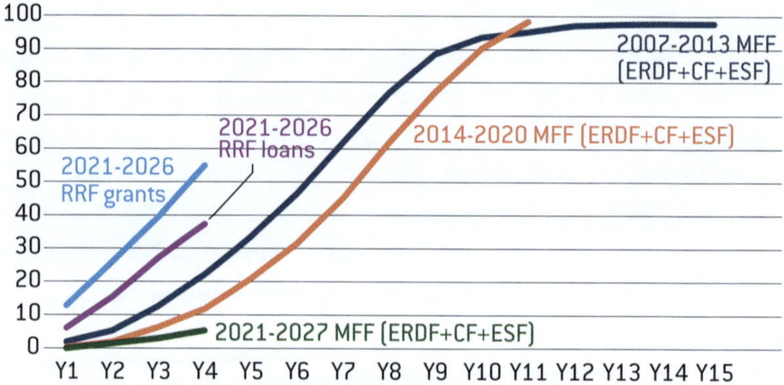

Source: Bruegel based on the European Commission's Cohesion Data Space and RRF scoreboard. Note: Year 1 is the first year of the respective programme, ie 2007 for the 2007-2013 MFF, 2014 for the 2014-2020 MFF, and 2021 for the 2021-2027 MFF and the RRF. The figure does not include values for the incomplete year 2025. As of 3 July 2025, absorption rates were 98.9 percent for the 2014-2020 MFF, 9.8 percent for the 2021-2027 MFF, 57.4 percent for the 2021-2026 RRF grants and 38.2 percent for the 2021-2026 RRF loans.

Table 10: Total planned disbursements from the three main cohesion funds and the RRF by country (€ billions)

	2014-2020 MFF (ERDF+CF+ESF)	2021-2027 MFF (ERDF+CF+ESF)	2021-2026 RRF grants	2021-2026 RRF loans
Austria	1.25	0.93	3.96	---
Belgium	2.21	2.32	5.03	0.24
Bulgaria	7.81	9.51	5.69	---
Croatia	8.91	8.52	5.79	4.25
Cyprus	0.84	0.87	1.02	0.20
Czechia	22.65	19.41	8.41	0.82
Denmark	0.63	0.37	1.63	---
Estonia	3.70	3.02	0.95	---
Finland	1.48	1.47	1.95	---
France	17.78	15.75	40.27	---
Germany	20.67	17.38	30.33	---
Greece	17.75	19.17	18.22	17.73
Hungary	22.43	21.47	6.51	3.92
Ireland	1.03	0.90	1.15	---
Italy	46.00	41.15	71.78	122.60
Latvia	4.58	4.24	1.97	---
Lithuania	6.97	6.00	2.29	1.55
Luxembourg	0.18	0.03	0.24	---
Malta	0.83	0.75	0.33	---
Netherlands	1.58	0.92	5.44	---
Poland	78.26	71.61	25.28	34.54
Portugal	23.09	22.38	16.33	5.89
Romania	23.77	28.85	13.57	14.93
Slovakia	14.12	12.13	6.41	---
Slovenia	3.32	2.98	1.61	1.07
Spain	42.07	34.69	79.85	83.16
Sweden	2.02	1.57	3.45	---

Source: Bruegel based on the European Commission's Cohesion Data Space and RRF scoreboard.

4.3 Performance instruments in the current MFF

The current (2021-27) MFF has multiple headings, each containing various funds with varying approaches to disbursement, governance and alignment with overarching EU objectives. There is no unified framework for assessing the impact of the MFF as a whole.

However, building on the perceived success of the RRF, certain performance elements were introduced into the Common Agricultural Policy (CAP) from 2023. These changes, however, have been criticised. Cohesion policy already includes a performance framework, which in some respects is more detailed than that of the RRF.

In addition to performance, the EU budget incorporates mainstreaming mechanisms to ensure that horizontal priorities are integrated into all spending programmes.

This section examines these three aspects: performance in the CAP, cohesion policy and the horizontal mainstreaming of EU-wide policy priorities.

4.3.1 The CAP performance framework falls short

The CAP has long consumed a large share of the EU budget. Historically, it focused on securing the food supply, enhancing agricultural productivity and ensuring a high living standard in the agricultural sector through redistribution (Kengyel, 2022). In recent years, its goals have expanded to include environmental and climate sustainability.

However, the way CAP disburses funds highlights the limited role of performance-based budgeting. Most funds are distributed to farmers through direct income support, primarily based on farm size. While this model supports farm incomes, it has also led to dependency and reduced efficiency (Pe'er *et al*, 2017). From an environmental perspective, WWF (2024) found that 58 percent to 60 percent of CAP spending is harmful to biodiversity.

To tackle these problems, the Commission has introduced reforms, which came into effect in 2023, aiming for a *"fairer, greener and more performance-based CAP"*[40]. The reforms in principle attach to the disbursement of funds reinforced conditions related to minimising harmful farming practices and the introduction of voluntary eco-schemes, which provide additional funds to farms with sustainable practices. The reform also introduced country-level CAP strategic plans, which aim to increase policy coherence across CAP funds, while allowing EU countries to tailor them to local needs. The legislation also defines a common set of indicators, which will be monitored through annual performance reports and bi-annual reviews of plans. Some of these features echo aspects of the RRF framework.

However, the reforms were criticised even before they took effect. Pe'er *et al* (2022) argued that while EU countries have more flexibility to pursue green goals, many show reluctance to implement them. Kengyel (2022) warned that with greater national control and weaker EU oversight, the greening of the CAP now depends heavily on national-level commitments, and that existing safeguards are too weak. Guyomard *et al* (2024) highlighted that many EU countries have chosen economic objectives over environmental ones in their plans, also noting that economic objectives do not currently address the disadvantages of direct income support.

Criticisms were also raised by the European Court of Auditors, which found that plans for 2023-2027 are greener than in the previous CAP period, but do not match the EU's ambitions for the climate and the environment (ECA, 2024a). They also noted that key elements for assessing green performance are missing. While the Commission aims to use result indicators, many are in fact output-based. In addition, the ECA (2024a) found that of 24 indicators (13 of which are mandatory), only seven were used by EU members in their plans. Overall, final plans do not show a substantial increase in green ambition (ECA,

40 See 'The common agricultural policy: 2023-27', European Commission, https://agriculture.ec.europa.eu/common-agricultural-policy/cap-overview/cap-2023-27_en.

2024a). While recent CAP reforms have moved policies away from unconditional income support towards a more nuanced system, direct income support remains the most used policy tool[41].

The use of performance indicators in the CAP framework differs significantly from their use under the RRF. Under the RRF, funds are disbursed only after milestones and targets are met. While the new CAP framework theoretically allows for payments to be withheld, Guyomard *et al* (2024) argued that such corrective measures are unlikely to be applied before 2027. They also suggested that the new setup increases the administrative burden, with limited impact on the actual achievement of the CAP's stated objectives.

The shift to national strategic plans, which are assessed at EU level, has created the opportunity for performance-based budgeting. However, in its actual implementation, the uptake of result indicators in national strategic plans is still lacking. While setting clear indicators could foster more climate and environmental measures, redistribution goals are more challenging to integrate into a performance-based budgeting approach.

We thus conclude that a shift to national CAP plans can open up possibilities for performance-based budgeting. However, to realise this potential, the framework must include mandatory result-oriented performance indicators, applicable to all EU countries.

CAP greening has been met with significant push-back, as shown by widespread farmers' protests in 2024. If the reform of the current subsidy system towards a more performance-based framework that effectively reduces emissions is not possible, the EU will have to use alternative policy tools to decarbonise the agricultural sector. For example, Denmark has called for the EU-wide inclusion of the agricultural sector in the EU emissions trading system (ETS) (Guyomard *et al*, 2024), while taxing carbon emissions from the agricultural sector

41 See 'CAP at a glance', European Commission, https://agriculture.ec.europa.eu/common-agricultural-policy/cap-overview/cap-glance_en.

(for example from livestock or peatland drained for farming use; see Box 2 in chapter 3).

4.3.2 Cohesion policy: mostly performance-oriented, yet at risk of policy overload

Cohesion policy has long been a cornerstone of European integration, with economic convergence as a key priority. It is also one of the largest components of the EU budget, underlining its significance in EU policymaking. In its mid-term review of cohesion policy, published April 2025, the European Commission highlighted the policy's role in contributing to new political priorities[42].

Cohesion policy has also been one of the most controversial budget items and, despite various reforms, continues to face criticism (Zeitlin *et al*, 2023). Criticisms include difficulties in monitoring performance because of the diversity of objectives and concerns about the reliability of evaluation studies, related to the lack of independence of national authorities and the European Commission (Schout, 2024). Recent efforts have tried to push cohesion policy towards a more performance-based approach. Begg *et al* (2024) noted that under the current MFF, cohesion policy has shifted to a stronger results orientation, with the shift away from a 'financing-linked-to-cost' approach fundamental to this reform.

Begg *et al* (2025a) argued that current cohesion policy uses a mix of input, output and result indicators. Unlike the RRF, the various cohesion fund regulations define standardised indicators to be used by EU countries, enabling comprehensive and targeted monitoring of both outputs and results. Begg *et al* (2025a) also argued that performance evaluation under cohesion policy is quite advanced, as it involves continuous assessments (ie before, during and after implementation). Thus, cohesion policy seems to be the EU budget instrument most

42 See 'A modernised Cohesion policy: The mid-term review', European Commission, https://ec.europa.eu/regional_policy/information-sources/publications/communications/2025/a-modernised-cohesion-policy-the-mid-term-review_en.

aligned with performance-based budgeting, under the current MFF.

However, the attempt to leverage cohesion policy to achieve additional EU policy objectives, as envisioned under mainstreaming (section 4.3.3) may put its core policy objective at risk. Bachtler and Wostner (2025) argued that cohesion policy has become overburdened with multiple policy objectives and call for it to be refocused back onto its primary objective of economic convergence. In contrast, the European Commission's mid-term review aims to broaden the scope of cohesion policy to the financing of new political priorities, such as defence. Critics argue that this shift in priorities makes cohesion policy an instrument of current political agendas, potentially undermining its foundational objective of fostering economic convergence across EU regions[43].

Our review of the performance frameworks under CAP and cohesion policy yielded contrasting insights. The 2023 CAP reform introduced national strategic plans and a performance monitoring system inspired by the RRF. However, the early evidence suggests the reforms have had a limited effect. The CAP's continued reliance on direct income support linked to farm size, the broad and overly generous classification of climate-related spending and weak enforcement mechanisms have contributed to environmental greenwashing and undermined performance credibility. Even though the CAP now formally allows performance corrections, they are unlikely to be applied before 2027, and the administrative burden of the reforms appears to outweigh their effectiveness. Cohesion policy, by contrast, is the most performance-oriented budget line under the current MFF. It includes a mix of input, output and result indicators and applies continuous performance monitoring before, during and after implementation. The use of common indicators across EU members has improved comparability and allowed for some degree of policy learning.

43 See CEMR, 'Cohesion Policy Mid-Term Review,' 15 April 2025, https://ccre-cemr.org/impactgoal-cohesion/cohesion-policy-mid-term-review.

However, cohesion policy faces three major risks. First, concerns about the fraudulent use of funds undermine the policy's credibility. Second, reputational and governance challenges persist because of concerns about the independence of evaluation and the complexity of implementation. And third, cohesion policy is at risk of being overburdened with new political priorities, from climate goals to defence spending. This mission creep could ultimately weaken its effectiveness, particularly if funding is not aligned with regional development objectives.

4.3.3 EU budget mainstreaming needs reform

In principle, the EU budget should support the achievement of EU-wide horizontal priorities, in relation to issues such as climate change, biodiversity, gender equality, the Sustainable Development Goals and the digital transition[44]. The process of incorporating these priorities into the budget is known as budgetary mainstreaming, meaning they should be embedded in all stages of the EU budget cycle, from design to implementation and evaluation.

The overarching targets are the allocation of 30 percent of the current MFF and 37 percent of the RRF to investments in climate change mitigation and adaptation. The MFF includes numerical targets for biodiversity spending (7.5 percent in 2024 and 10 percent in 2026 and 2027), while the RRF includes a digital spending target (20 percent). There are no quantitative targets for gender equality and the Sustainable Development Goals, and no digital target in the MFF.

These targets reflect commendable goals, but a closer look reveals significant concerns about the methodology used to calculate the climate impact of EU spending. Begg *et al* (2025a) and Darvas and Sekut (2025) found the methodology overly complex, incoherent and lacking

44 See 'Financing of horizontal policy priorities in the EU budget', European Commission, available at https://commission.europa.eu/strategy-and-policy/eu-budget/performance-and-reporting/horizontal-priorities_en.

transparency, leading to inconsistent application. Environmentally harmful activities are not accounted for, even though some EU countries report them in their national disclosures. As noted in section 4.3.1, WWF (2024) estimated that about 60 percent of CAP spending and other EU budget items negatively impact biodiversity.

A fundamental issue is the classification system, which assigns EU spending to just three coefficients: 0 percent, 40 percent and 100 percent. For most EU spending programmes, projects are classified into intervention fields to which these coefficients are assigned. Intervention fields with a 100 percent weight are considered crucial to climate goals (eg renewables, R&D), 40 percent indicates moderate impact and 0 percent signals no relevance.

However, intervention fields are often too broadly defined, potentially grouping together activities with very different climate impacts. The system's complexity leads to inconsistent application and the basis for assigning coefficients is often unclear, raising doubts about the reliability of aggregated climate spending figures (Darvas and Sekut, 2025).

The risk of overstating positive climate impacts, while ignoring harmful activities, is particularly acute in CAP spending. CAP expenditures are not broken down into detailed intervention fields but classified into just four broad categories, each assigned either 40 percent or 100 percent coefficients. These generous classifications significantly overstate the CAP's climate contribution and, by extension, the climate relevance of the EU budget overall – amounting to what some officials interviewed by Begg *et al* (2025a) described as greenwashing.

The European Court of Auditors has reviewed the climate and digital mainstreaming targets of the RRF and found mixed results. While the 37 percent climate spending target was reportedly exceeded, the methodology used to calculate this figure may have led to an overestimation of actual green spending. Moreover, assessing the real impact was challenging because of the absence of adequate tracking systems (ECA, 2024b). On digital objectives, the European Court of

Auditors found that, while EU countries met or even surpassed the 20 percent spending target, this spending often lacked strategic alignment and did not effectively support the EU's broader digital transformation goals (ECA, 2025a).

4.4 Conclusions

The new conceptual foundation of the next MFF, as outlined by the European Commission in February 2025, is a welcome initiative, particularly in how it distinguishes between spending areas directly managed by the Commission (pillar two on competitiveness and pillar three on external action) and those primarily overseen by member states (pillar one, including agriculture and cohesion policy). The proposal to introduce a performance framework for the latter is also welcome.

Some of the additional EU spending needs we have identified in chapter 2 would align well with this framework. For example, environmental action could be integrated into pillar one, while international climate finance fits naturally under pillar three. However, other elements, such as cross-border infrastructure, do not fit as easily within this structure and risk under-provision if left unaddressed. These types of EPG could either be incorporated into pillar one, provided that a minimum threshold for cross-border projects is established for national plans to encourage intergovernmental cooperation, or be placed within a newly established fourth pillar dedicated to EPGs not currently covered by the Competitiveness Fund or the External Action Fund.

Establishing a performance framework for pillar one is well justified, because spending managed by countries is subject to moral hazard, as beneficiaries who apply for funding often possess private information about the true social value of their projects. Requiring the fulfilment of specific performance indicators within a structured performance framework can help ensure better project selection and will enable the Commission to monitor whether spending aligns with the EU's strategic goals and delivers European added value.

However, the current EU budgetary architecture to foster

performance and strategic alignment suffers from various weaknesses. To realise the potential of performance-based budgeting, deeper reform is needed – both in relation to how funds are allocated and how their effectiveness is measured. The next MFF cycle will be an opportunity to address these structural weaknesses and institutionalise the lessons from the RRF, CAP, cohesion policy and mainstreaming.

As the RRF may serve as a template for the performance framework of pillar one in the next MFF, we have identified several shortcomings that should be addressed in future performance-based frameworks. To be effective, such a framework will have to include indicators that are genuinely results-based, rather than relying heavily on input and output indicators[45]. National plans should be structured similarly and use a standardised set of indicators for comparability.

The negotiation process for national plans should be transparent and local stakeholders should be involved meaningfully in both the design and evaluation of the plans. National plans should be comparable across countries to ensure accountability, particularly in relation to EU added value and ambition.

The negotiation and implementation process should not be rushed. Timelines for implementation and absorption of funds must be designed with sufficient flexibility to account for differing national capacities and changing circumstances.

Important lessons should be learned from the performance-based frameworks of cohesion and agricultural policies. In particular, though the cohesion policy framework offers valuable insights into design of effective performance-based systems, it suffers from some shortcomings. The CAP framework appears unlikely to deliver meaningful performance improvements. Setting numerical targets for reducing harmful emissions and enhancing biodiversity as

45 Input and output indicators should still be included in a performance-based framework, since completing projects and thus achieving results may take time, while interim financing is generally needed before project completion. Result indicators, however, should be prominent.

preconditions for agricultural policy financing could significantly strengthen the public good aspect of this policy. These targets should be established regardless of whether our recommendation made in chapter 2 to shift agricultural subsidies to national budgets is adopted, or if such subsidies stay with the EU budget.

With a more streamlined approach for the EU budget, mainstreaming will become an important tool in advancing horizontal policy objectives. However, we found that the current framework is inadequate and requires substantial revision to avoid the effectiveness of spending being misrepresented. In particular, tracking systems should be overhauled to follow a transparent and robust methodology that accurately reflects the potential impact of investments.

5 Preparing the EU budget for enlargement

5.1 Context

Russia's full-scale invasion of Ukraine in 2022 significantly altered geopolitical risk assessments and injected new momentum into the European Union enlargement process, not only for Ukraine, but also for Moldova, Georgia and the Western Balkans[46]. As EU candidate countries[47] have economies that are considerably poorer than the EU average (in GDP *per capita* at purchasing power parity terms; Table 11), they are expected to become major beneficiaries of EU cohesion policy when they do join. Ukraine's agricultural lands are equal to one-fourth of the agricultural area of current EU members (Table 11) and thus Ukraine is expected to be a major beneficiary of the Common Agricultural Policy (CAP). This has led to exaggerated concerns that enlargement could impose an excessive financial burden on current member states and could turn several current net beneficiaries into net payers (Kribbe and van Middelaar, 2023).

46 The enlargement process with Türkiye remains stalled.

47 Kosovo's current status is 'potential candidate'. Its EU accession process is hindered by its international recognition as an independent state, as five EU countries (Cyprus, Greece, Romania, Slovakia and Spain) do not recognise it. Kosovo's Stabilisation and Associating Agreement with the EU is in force since April 2016.

Table 11: Key dates in the EU accession process and population sizes, development levels and agricultural areas of candidate countries

	EU membership application	Official EU candidate status	Decision to start accession negotiations	Start of accession negotiations	Population (millions, 2024)	GDP *per capita* at PPP (% EU, 2024)	Agricultural land area (% EU)
Albania	Apr-2009	Jun-2014	Mar-2020	Jul-2022	2.7	35	0.7
Bosnia and Herzegovina	Feb-2016	Dec-2022	Mar-2024	---	3.5	35	1.4
Georgia	Mar-2022	Dec-2023	---	---	3.7	45	1.5
Kosovo	Dec-2022	---	---	---	1.6	30	0.3
Moldova	Mar-2022	Jun-2022	Dec-2023	Jun-2024	2.4	30	1.4
Montenegro	Dec-2008	Dec-2010	Dec-2011	Jun-2012	0.6	51	0.2
North Macedonia	Mar-2004	Dec-2005	Mar-2020	Jul-2022	1.8	44	0.8
Serbia	Dec-2009	Mar-2012	Jun-2013	Jan-2014	6.6	50	2.1
Ukraine	Feb-2022	Jun-2022	Dec-2023	Jun-2024	33.3	32	25.4

Sources: Bruegel based on European Commission country pages for the EU accession process dates; IMF World Economic Outlook April 2025 database for population and GDP *per capita*; FAO for agricultural land. Note: data on agricultural land for Kosovo is not available. We therefore approximated it as 40 percent of Kosovo's total area, based on the average (39 percent) and median (41 percent) ratios of agricultural land to total area in the other five Western Balkan countries.

In this chapter, we argue that the direct financial burden of enlargement would be manageable for current EU members, even in a highly unlikely scenario in which all nine candidate countries join the EU by 2030, with no changes to EU budget rules and no transitional periods (which typically limit certain EU payments to new members). However, it's unlikely that all nine candidates will join in the next few years, while budgetary rules will likely change in the 2028-2034 Multiannual Financial Framework (MFF) and in any case transitional periods will likely apply (in the past three enlargement rounds – 2004, 2007 and 2013 – it took about ten years for new members to fully benefit from EU-funded programmes). We set out a hypothetical transition scenario based on these three enlargement rounds, and estimate an upper limit for the direct cost of enlargement to the EU budget for the 2028-2034 MFF.

Moreover, any comprehensive cost-benefit analysis should take into consideration the broader fiscal advantages that may accrue to current EU countries as a result of future enlargements. The forthcoming eastern accessions are likely to reflect the pattern seen in previous eastern enlargement rounds, which generated substantial benefits for companies in existing member states and contributed to higher GDP growth and increased tax revenues in existing members, thereby reducing the fiscal impact of enlargement for national governments.

5.2 The difficulty of estimating the budgetary impact of enlargement

Numerous uncertainties surround estimates of the budgetary impact of prospective EU enlargements on the 2028-2034 EU MFF (Darvas *et al*, 2024; Rubio *et al*, 2025). These include uncertainty about when accessions will happen, the design and duration of transitional arrangements, the rules governing EU budget allocations and geopolitical developments. In particular, the resolution of the war in Ukraine, and Ukraine's post-conflict characteristics in terms of population size, GDP and agricultural land area, will significantly affect the country's potential entitlements from the EU budget. Moreover, it remains unclear whether the spending ceilings in the next MFF will be increased to accommodate new members. As a result, no reliable estimate can currently be made of the impact of prospective enlargement on the next MFF.

Nevertheless, potential impacts on the EU budget can be estimated on the basis that no transition periods and unchanged allocation rules are assumed, and alternative scenarios for Ukraine's post-war recovery are evaluated. For instance, Darvas *et al* (2024) assessed two scenarios for Ukraine: one in which the country fully regains its pre-war territory, population and GDP, and another in which each of these factors is reduced by 20 percent. The first scenario, when combined with unchanged budgetary rules, no transition periods and the accession of all nine candidate countries in 2028, provides an upper-bound estimate of the potential impact of enlargement on the EU budget (Darvas and Mejino-López, 2024; Rubio *et al*, 2025).

Assuming continuation of the current budgetary allocation rules and structure, there are two alternative approaches to quantifying the budgetary impact of enlargement. One approach, followed by Rubio *et al* (2025), assumed that the overall size of the EU budget remains unchanged, implying that current EU members will see reductions in their allocations from the budget across all budget headings, in order to accommodate payments to new members. The authors justify their assumption by noting that the overall EU budget did not expand during the previous three rounds of eastern enlargement. The alternative approach, used by Darvas and Mejino-López (2024), assumed that funding for new members would be added on top of the allocations received by the current 27 members, resulting in an overall increase in the size of the EU budget. Darvas and Mejino-López (2024) based their assumption on the premise of unchanged allocation rules, since a shrinking envelope for current EU members could not be achieved unless rules are changed, particularly in the two largest spending areas, agriculture and cohesion, which together account for more than two-thirds of the MFF.

Despite these differing assumptions, both approaches lead to qualitatively similar conclusions. Assuming a larger overall budget implies a somewhat higher estimated cost of enlargement, as a fixed-size budget would necessitate smaller overall payments, including to new members who would be net beneficiaries, thereby reducing the net fiscal impact.

5.3 An estimate of the EU budget impact of enlargement

The first step in estimating the upper bound of the potential impact of enlargement on the next MFF, starting in 2028, is to quantify a hypothetical scenario in which the nine candidate countries are incorporated into the MFF under unchanged budgetary rules. The calculations by Darvas and Mejino-López (2024) are based on current EU budget rules, with one exception: the overall upper limits on EU spending are not applied.

Cohesion policy is the only area of EU spending governed by a specific allocation methodology, which is partly based on GDP *per capita* relative to the EU average. Since the inclusion of lower-income candidate countries would reduce the EU's average GDP *per capita*, several current EU countries would receive less cohesion funding under unchanged rules. For all other categories of EU spending, it is assumed that current EU countries would continue to receive the same amounts as currently.

Spending allocated to the nine new member states, along with related expenditures such as higher administrative costs, is added on top of the actual 2021-2027 MFF. As a result, all but one of the MFF headings would increase with enlargement. The only exception would be neighbourhood policy spending, which decreases because the candidate countries, once they become EU members, would no longer be eligible for funding under this category[48]. For cohesion policy, current allocation rules are applied in detail to estimate how much

48 EU neighbourhood spending in countries other than the nine candidates is assumed to continue.

funding the new members would receive. For other spending categories, including the CAP, allocations are assumed to be proportional to those received by the 13 countries that joined the EU between 2004 and 2013. Proportionality is based on agricultural land area for CAP allocations and on GDP and population for other categories. The expected contributions of the nine new members to the EU budget are also taken into account.

The analysis uses population and GDP data and projections from 2020 – the year when the 2021-2027 MFF was finalised. These figures do not reflect the impact of the war in Ukraine, which has severely damaged Ukraine's economy, reduced its population and resulted in the occupation of parts of its territory. For the purposes of this scenario, it is assumed that Ukraine will regain its territorial integrity and that the war will have no lasting effect on its population or GDP. If Ukraine were to experience permanent losses in territory, population or economic output, the net transfers it would receive from the EU budget would be lower than what we estimate[49].

5.3.1 Impact on the size of the budget

Our calculations indicate that the MFF would increase from its overall 2021-2027 size of €1,211 billion to €1,356 billion, or from 1.12 percent to 1.23 percent of EU GDP, as a result of enlargement (Table 12).

49 See the annex of Darvas and Mejino-López (2024) for further methodological details.

Table 12: Approved expenditures under the 2021-2027 MFF and a hypothetical budget including nine new countries (current prices, € billions)

	Approved budget	Hypothetical budget with nine new countries		
	EU27	EU36	EU27	New 9
Cohesion policy	393	422	361	61
Common Agricultural Policy	379	491	379	113
Neighbourhood and the world	111	96		
European public administration	82	89		
Others	246	258	246	12
Total	**1,211**	**1,356**		
% GDP	1.12	1.23		

Source: Bruegel.

Cohesion spending for the current EU would drop from €393 billion to €361 billion as a result of the downward adjustment in allocations caused by the enlargement-induced decline in average EU GDP *per capita*[50]. The nine new EU members would receive an estimated €61 billion in cohesion funding, raising total cohesion expenditures to €422 billion. CAP spending for the current EU would remain unchanged at

50 The reduced cohesion spending in current EU members results from regional reclassification. The EU's regions are classified as less developed (regional GDP per capita below 75 percent of the EU average), transition (between 75 percent and 100 percent) and more developed (above 100 percent). Enlargement would lower the overall EU average GDP per capita, causing some current less-developed EU regions to shift to transition status, and some transition regions to shift to more-developed status. This reclassification would result in reduced cohesion funding for affected regions.

€379 billion (as per our assumption), while the inclusion of €113 billion in CAP allocations for the nine new countries would raise the total CAP budget to €491 billion.

Neighbourhood policy spending would drop by €15 billion, as the new members would no longer be eligible for such funding. By contrast, spending on European public administration would increase by €7 billion to reflect the administrative costs associated with enlargement. All other spending categories directed at current EU countries are assumed to remain unchanged, while the nine new countries would receive an additional €12 billion from these categories.

5.3.2 The net cost and its impact on net positions from the MFF

The nine prospective EU countries would be net beneficiaries from the EU budget. The net cost to current EU countries resulting from the accession of these nine countries is estimated at €180 billion (in current prices) over the MFF period, equivalent to approximately €26 billion per year, or 0.17 percent of EU GDP.

This additional cost would have only a modest impact on EU members' net budgetary positions with the EU budget. Several current net beneficiaries, including Hungary, Bulgaria, Latvia, Lithuania, Greece, Romania, Poland, Czechia, Slovenia and Malta, already experienced significant reductions in the net transfers they received from the EU budget during 2021-2023, compared to the 2014-2020 MFF (Figure 8). For these countries, any further reduction in net transfers resulting from a new enlargement wave would likely be relatively small in comparison to the cuts already incurred.

For the net contributors, the enlargement would require an additional contribution to the EU budget equivalent to approximately 0.13 percent of their GDP to finance the integration of the new members.

Figure 8: Net balances with the EU budget (% GNI)

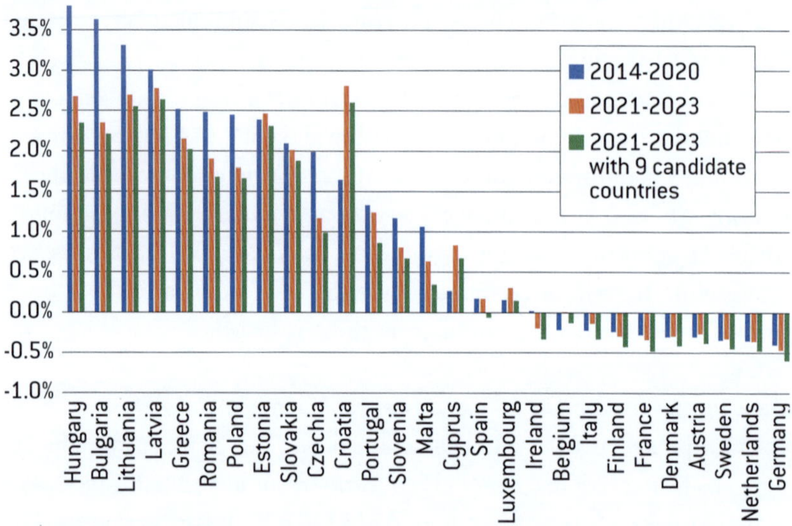

Source: Bruegel based on European Commission data. Note: EU budget expenditures = all allocations to countries excluding European public administration. Expenditures in non-EU countries, other earmarked items, European public administration and NGEU-related spending are not included. Revenues = total national contributions but not customs duties, sugar levies, fines, other revenues and EU borrowing to finance NGEU.

5.4 The impact of possible transition periods

Previous EU enlargement rounds involved various transition periods, not only for labour mobility but also for integration into EU policies with budgetary implications. Whether similar transition arrangements will apply in the upcoming enlargement rounds – and what specific features they will include – will be determined in the accession negotiations between current and prospective EU members.

In our calculations, we calibrate a transition scenario for integration into the EU budget based on the experience of the last three eastern enlargement rounds (2004, 2007 and 2013). As shown in Figure 9, while the new members began making full contributions to the EU budget from their accession dates, EU spending in these countries increased only gradually. For the 2004 entrants, it took approximately ten years to reach peak transfers from the EU budget; for Bulgaria and Romania, this process took eight years; and for Croatia, seven years. In the first full calendar year after EU entry, the 2024 new members obtained 39 percent of their peak payments, Bulgaria and Romania obtained 31 percent, while Croatia obtained 25 percent. These values reflect actual outcomes and EU spending in the new members also depended on their capacity to absorb funds, but these patterns nonetheless provide a useful indication of what might be expected in future eastern enlargement rounds.

Figure 9: EU budget expenditures in central European new members and their contributions to the EU budget, % GNI, 2000-2023

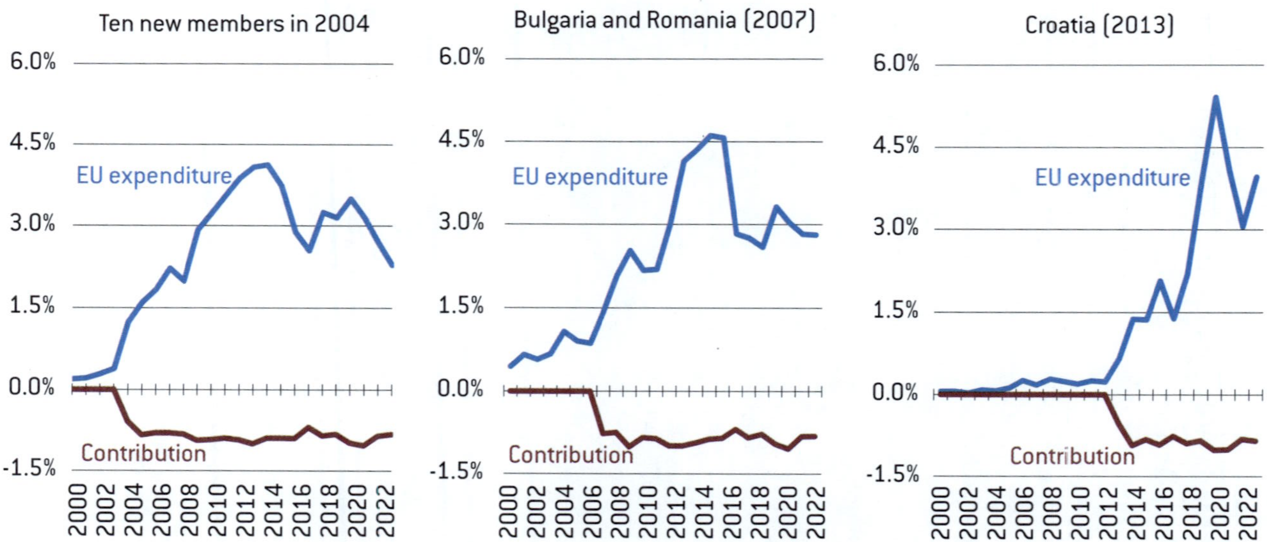

Source: Bruegel based on European Commission data. Note: the 2004 enlargement was on 1 May, and Croatia's accession was on 1 July, not in January, and therefore 2004 and 2013 were not full calendar years of EU membership for the new members that joined in those years.

To estimate an upper-bound scenario for the impact of prospective enlargements on the next MFF from 2028-2034, we make the following assumptions.

- All nine candidate countries join the EU on 1 January 2030.
- In 2030, the first year of EU membership, EU allocations to new members amount to 40 percent of their long-term value.
- The transition period for their full integration into EU budget spending lasts seven years – the shortest observed duration among the 2004-2013 enlargements. Thus, we assume that the disbursement of EU funds to new members ramps up gradually over the transition period, from 40 percent of the long-term value in 2030 to 100 percent in 2036.
- Consistent with previous rounds, we assume that the new members begin making full contributions to the EU budget from the date of their accession.
- Similarly to current EU members that obtained funding from the EU budget before their entry, we assume that new members obtain 10 percent of their long-term funding value in 2028 and 20 percent in 2029, but would not contribute to the EU budget in these two years.
- The reduction for current members of EU neighbourhood spending and cohesion spending, and the increase in EU public administration spending, occur from 2030.
- We assume a 3 percent nominal GDP growth rate (for all EU countries, including the new members) to calculate current price values.

With these assumptions, we estimate the net cost of enlargement to the current 27 EU members, paid via the 2028-2034 MFF, at €107 billion (in current prices) in total over seven years, equivalent to approximately 0.08 percent of their combined GNIs. However, it is highly unlikely that actual costs will approach this level. First, it is extremely improbable that all nine candidate countries will join the EU in 2030. Second, EU budgetary rules are likely to evolve, particularly in ways that reduce net payments to less-affluent members – an adjustment already observed in the transition from the 2014–2020 MFF to the 2021–2027 MFF. Third, our assumptions are conservative, as we took the shortest transition period (seven years) and the highest initial payment rate (40 percent) from the historical precedents.

5.5 Fiscal benefits of enlargement for current members beyond the EU budget

It is important to distinguish between the net budgetary cost to current EU governments, ie their increased contributions to the EU budget, and the net fiscal cost, or the impact of enlargement on national budgets. National budgets would benefit from increased tax revenues and social-security contributions resulting from the accession of the nine candidate countries.

Enlargement expands the European single market, creating new trade, investment and labour mobility opportunities. The eastern enlargements of 2004, 2007 and 2013 provide ample evidence of such effects, having generated substantial gains for both new and old members, driven by increased trade integration, capital flows and institutional convergence (Campos *et al*, 2019).

Firms in current EU members benefit not only from increased market access, but also from participation in EU-financed programmes in the new members. Crucitti *et al* (2023) concluded that western and northern EU countries in particular benefited from spillovers from EU cohesion policy spending in central and eastern European (CEE) member states, Benefits were felt especially by those countries with strong trade links to the region, such as Austria.

EU accession is also expected to stimulate foreign direct investment (FDI) inflows into the new members. Prior enlargement rounds have demonstrated that EU membership boosts investor confidence by reducing regulatory uncertainty and improving the rule of law. FDI flows from western to central and eastern Europe increased significantly after 2004, often leading to technology transfer, productivity gains and stronger value chain integration (Medve-Bálint, 2014). A similar pattern is likely to emerge with the accession of the Western Balkan countries and Ukraine, Moldova and Georgia, especially given their infrastructure development needs.

In addition, enlargement facilitates labour mobility. Migrant workers from new members can help alleviate labour shortages in key sectors across the EU, including healthcare, construction and agriculture. Evidence from the 2004 enlargement suggests that labour mobility contributed to economic dynamism in receiving countries, while also generating fiscal revenues through income taxes and social security contributions (Dustmann *et al*, 2010).

Taken together, these effects are expected to support higher economic growth, employment and corporate profitability in current EU countries, leading to higher national fiscal revenues. These fiscal gains can compensate, or at least partly offset, the net contributions required to finance enlargement through the EU budget.

5.6 Conclusion

The potential enlargement of the EU to include nine new members poses legitimate questions about the fiscal implications for current members. However, the analysis presented in this chapter suggests that the direct budgetary costs are likely to be manageable. Even under the most conservative assumptions - immediate accession, no transitional arrangements and unchanged budget rules - the estimated net cost to current members would represent 0.13 percent of GDP on average, a modest share. If all nine candidates become EU members in 2030, and based on conservative assumptions about transition periods, the direct financial burden could amount to 0.08 percent EU GDP. However, it is unlikely that all nine candidates will join in 2030 and budgetary rules will likely change to mitigate the fiscal pressures.

Moreover, a narrow focus on EU budget contributions overlooks the wider macroeconomic and fiscal benefits of enlargement. Past accessions have consistently delivered gains in trade, investment, labour mobility and tax revenues for existing members. These dynamic effects are expected to play out again with future enlargements. The challenge is not affordability but of institutional readiness to adapt the EU budget framework to a larger EU.

6 Policy implications and recommendations

In this Blueprint, we have evaluated the alignment of current EU spending with the concept of European public goods (EPGs) and examined the optimum contribution the EU budget could make to meeting the EU's most pressing spending needs. We have also outlined the main principles when thinking about new sources of revenue for the EU budget and have evaluated various proposals. We have examined how the EU could move more towards performance-based funding, and have assessed the potential impact of future EU enlargements on the 2028-2034 MFF.

We concluded that only about half of current EU spending goes to EPGs (chapter 2). Another significant portion supports cohesion: a policy preference involving redistribution from richer to poorer countries that cannot be nationalised. But other non-EPG EU spending amounting to about 0.3 percent of GNI should be shifted to national budgets, freeing up EU resources for EPGs. Even in this case, the EU budget would remain too small to accommodate the 0.9 percent of GDP in additional spending needed to fully fund EPGs. Moreover, the EU still lacks a dedicated budgetary instrument to address in a timely and coordinated manner large-scale crises that demand joint spending, such as pandemics or migration surges.

We recommend the following measures in relation to the composition and volume of EU spending:

- Focus the MFF on the provision of genuine EPGs, such as climate action, research, competitiveness, cross-border infrastructure and security.
- Expand the size of the MFF to 1.7 percent of GNI if 0.3 percent

of current non-EPG spending, including agricultural subsidies, is shifted to the national level. While rules governing the EU's Common Agricultural Policy (CAP) should continue to be set at EU level, funding of its non-EPG components should move to national budgets.

- If shifting non-EPG spending to the national level proves politically impossible, the size of the MFF must be increased to 2 percent of GNI to accommodate additional spending needs that would be best implemented at EU level.
- Separate consideration is required for the contribution of the EU budget to boosting the EU's defence capabilities. While certain measures, such as defence industrial policy and incentives for common procurement, could be financed by the MFF – and thus the MFF should increase beyond the 1.7 percent to 2.0 percent of GNI range mentioned above – others, such as common purchases of strategic defence enablers, might need to be funded through an intergovernmental instrument.
- Establish an emergency crisis-response fund, possibly outside the MFF, to mobilise EU resources rapidly during emergencies, such as pandemics, without diverting funds from core EPG spending. A procedure should be put in place to secure fast mobilisation and implementation of the fund, possibly based on a European Council decision. Borrowing appears to be the appropriate funding mechanism for such an emergency fund, similar to NGEU.

Any increase in the MFF's size would ultimately be financed through transfers from EU members. Therefore, from the perspective of the total additional funds raised, the choice between introducing new revenue-raising mechanisms (new own resources) or increasing GNI-based contributions is immaterial (chapter 3). Even for revenues that EU members cannot raise individually, such as carbon border adjustment mechanism (CBAM) receipts, it is up to national governments to decide what share to keep and what share to allocate to the EU budget. In this sense, any transfer to the EU budget represents an opportunity cost for EU members. However, new revenue sources for the EU budget alter the cross-country distribution of contributions.

The main justifications for introducing new revenue sources should be to help achieve EU policy objectives (for example, increasing recycling through the plastic waste levy) and to weaken the dominance of the net-balance logic in EU budget debates.

We recommend the following actions to strengthen the revenue side of the EU budget:

- Allocate to the EU budget all customs duty revenues, and the proposed revenues arising from CBAM and the emissions trading system (ETS), except for a small collection cost (of up to about 2 percent). Directing to the EU budget revenues from activities within the EU's competence under the current Treaty framework would be politically legitimate.
- Consider climate-related levies on the aviation and maritime sectors, which are currently under-taxed, are responsible for significant shares of emissions and are difficult to regulate through national policies alone.
- Integrate agriculture into the ETS to accelerate decarbonisation of the sector while generating additional budget revenues.
- Establish external tax borders on corporate and personal income flows leaving the EU, and potentially also wealth. This would require tax-treaty policy to be harmonised or, at a minimum, rules that oblige EU countries to impose exit taxes on high-net-worth individuals who leave an EU country with unrealised capital gains.
- Consider dedicating EU budget revenue from the Under Taxed Profit Rule (UTPR) under Pillar Two of the OECD/G20 global tax agreement. The UTPR represents a collective European effort to enforce fair minimum taxation of multinational enterprises and protect the single market from tax avoidance by foreign firms.
- Adopt a defence spending shortfall levy to encourage low-

spending countries to increase their defence efforts and to partially compensate high-defence-spending countries by reducing their EU budget contributions. The EPG character of peace and security and the risk of free-riding by low-spending countries justify this levy.
- Eliminate *ad-hoc* rebates, which are inconsistent with the Fontainebleau principle that countries facing excessive budgetary burdens relative to their prosperity should be compensated, and which make EU budget contributions regressive. If elimination proves politically impossible, rebates should be replaced with a transparent, rules-based correction mechanism based on objective criteria tied to relative prosperity and contributions.

We also concluded that the European Commission's three-pillar outline for the next MFF is a welcome initiative (chapter 4). Some of the additional EU spending needs identified in chapter 2 would align well with this framework, but other elements, such as cross-border infrastructure, do not fit as easily within this structure and risk under-provision if left unaddressed. The proposal to introduce a performance framework for the first pillar, which includes activities primarily managed by EU countries on the basis of national plans, is a good suggestion.

While the Recovery and Resilience Facility (RRF) was a landmark tool to address the fallout from the pandemic and support the EU's twin transitions, it fell short of being a proper performance-based instrument. Therefore, the performance framework for pillar one of the next MFF should be designed to avoid the shortcomings of the RRF's performance approach. The main features of sound performance-based budgeting were missing from the RRF, including clear result indicators, transparent evaluation processes, comparability of national plans, adequate attention to cross-border projects, clarity on value for money and meaningful involvement of stakeholders beyond central governments in preparing and evaluating plans. Moreover, the European Commission's expanded role – covering design, negotiation, approval and evaluation of national plans, and evaluation of the overall impacts of the facility – creates a risk of conflicts of interest and could undermine objectivity. These shortcomings have important implications for the design of the performance framework for the first pillar of the next MFF, which envisages national plans in a performance-based setting to access funds, including cohesion and agricultural funds.

Other performance instruments in the current MFF also have weaknesses. The CAP's performance framework does not drive improvement effectively in the agricultural sector. Cohesion policy, while built on a standardised framework, faces reputational and governance challenges, concerns about fraudulent use of funds and the dilution of its effectiveness because of multiple competing priorities. Furthermore, the budgetary mainstreaming methodology has significant flaws and requires substantial revision to avoid misrepresenting the effectiveness of spending.

- EPGs related to cross-border infrastructure gaps could either be incorporated into pillar one of the next MFF, provided that a minimum threshold for cross-border projects is established for national plans, or be placed within a new fourth pillar dedicated to EPGs not currently covered by the Competitiveness Fund or the External Action Fund.
- Strengthen the design of performance-based budgeting by developing and requiring standardised result indicators in all national plans to enable meaningful comparisons and greater transparency.
- Ensure transparent negotiation processes for national plans and involve stakeholders meaningfully, including local stakeholders.
- Improve the objectivity of the European Commission's plan assessments through greater reliance on independent external evaluators.
- Avoid rushed implementation timelines; allow sufficient flexibility

to respond to unforeseen shocks while maintaining performance pressure.

- Align the CAP performance framework with the overall EU framework by introducing in all national plans mandatory result indicators that focus on emission reductions and the prevention of environmental and biodiversity degradation.
- Refocus cohesion policy on its core objective of economic convergence, underpinned by strong performance tracking, transparent evaluations and robust rule-of-law requirements.
- Overhaul the climate mainstreaming methodology by introducing a uniform, more granular classification system, applying negative coefficients to environmentally harmful spending and ensuring independent verification of reported impacts.
- Enhance mainstreaming of other horizontal priorities, such as gender equality, sustainable development goals and digitalisation, to meet the standards set for climate mainstreaming.

On enlargement (chapter 5) we concluded that the direct budgetary costs to the MFF would be manageable. Assuming all nine candidate countries join the EU by 2030, and applying conservative assumptions about transition periods, the direct financial burden could amount to about 0.08 percent of EU GDP. However, it is unlikely that all nine candidates will join in 2030, and budgetary rules will likely be adjusted to mitigate fiscal pressures. Moreover, a narrow focus on EU budget contributions overlooks the wider macroeconomic and fiscal benefits of enlargement. Past accessions have consistently delivered gains through increased trade, investment, labour mobility and tax revenues for existing members. These dynamic effects are expected to materialise again with future enlargements.

Our recommendations for preparing the next MFF for enlargement include:

- Plan for a gradually increasing and flexible enlargement budget by incorporating mechanisms into the 2028-2034 MFF that will allow incremental funding for new members, aligned with realistic accession timelines and absorption capacities.

- Update budget allocation rules to prevent significant reductions for current members when lower-income countries join. Allocation rules should be recalibrated to strike a balance between fairness and political feasibility.
- Increase the overall EU budget envelope to accommodate new members without reducing allocations for existing members. The necessary increase would be less than 0.08 percent of GDP if not all candidate countries join in 2030 and if budgetary rules are updated.
- Design structured transitional funding periods for new members to ensure smooth fiscal integration, and allow time for institutional adaptation.
- Communicate the broader fiscal and economic benefits of enlargement to EU citizens. Messaging should highlight the gains from past enlargements – including trade growth, FDI inflows and increased tax revenues in existing EU members – to counter concerns and misperceptions about net contributions and to build public support.

References

Aslam, A. and M. Delgado Coelho (2021) 'A Firm Lower Bound: Characteristics and Impact of Corporate Minimum Taxation,' *IMF Working Papers* 161, International Monetary Fund, available at https://doi.org/10.5089/9781513561073.001

Baccianti, C. (2022) 'The Public Spending Needs of Reaching the EU's Climate Targets,' in C. Floriana and S. Francesco (eds) *Greening Europe, 2022 European Public Investment Outlook*, Open Book Publishers, available at https://www.openbookpublishers.com/books/10.11647/obp.0328/chapters/10.11647/obp.0328.08

Bachtler, J., C. Mendez and R. Downes (2024) *Charting a new course for Cohesion Policy after 2027*, EoRPA Report 24/3, European Policies Research Centre, University of Strathclyde and EPRC Delft, available at https://eprc-strath.org/publication/charting-a-new-course-for-cohesion-policy-after-2027/

Bachtler, J. and P. Wostner (2025) 'Improving EU competitiveness within a reformed MFF and Cohesion Policy: directionality, alignment and leverage,' *European Policy Research Paper* 119, University of Strathclyde, available at https://eprc-strath.org/wp-content/uploads/2025/01/EPRP-119-2025-MFF_Competitiveness_Cohesion.pdf

Barake, M. and E. Le Pouhaër (2024) 'Tax revenue from Pillar One Amount A: country-by-country estimates,' *International Tax and Public Finance* 32: 680-740, available at https://doi.org/10.1007/s10797-024-09859-4

Barrett, S. (2007) *Why Cooperate?* Oxford University Press

Begg, I. (2008) 'Structural policy and economic convergence,' *CESifo Forum* 9(1): 3-9, ifo Institut für Wirtschaftsforschung an der Universität München, available at https://hdl.handle.net/10419/166313

Begg, I. (2009) *Fiscal Federalism, Subsidiarity and the EU Budget Review*, SIEPS 2009:1, Svenska institutet för europapolitiska studier, available at https://sieps.se/publikationer/2009/fiscal-federalism-subsidiarity-and-the-eu-budget-review/

Begg, I., F. Corti and A. Liscai (2024) *Performance framework for the EU*, Study requested by the BUDG Committee, European Parliament, available at https://www.europarl.europa.eu/RegData/etudes/STUD/2024/760700/IPOL_STU(2024)760700_EN.pdf

Begg, I., F. Corti, A. Liscai, Z. Darvas, M. Krystyanczuk, K. Sekut ... O. Van Der Valk (2025a) *Performance and mainstreaming framework for the EU budget - Empirical evidence, analysis and recommendations*, Study requested by the BUDG Committee, European Parliament, available at https://www.europarl.europa.eu/thinktank/en/document/IPOL_STU%282024%29767500

Begg, I., A. Liscai, Z. Darvas, A. Fiore, M. Krystyanczuk, K. Sekut ... O. Van Der Valk (2025b) *Performance-based Instruments: How could their design be improved?* Study requested by the CONT Committee, European Parliament, available at https://www.europarl.europa.eu/thinktank/en/document/BUDG_STU(2025)769432

Berith, R. (2017) 'European Public Goods in the Neo-Medieval Model of Governance', in S. Collignon (ed) *The Governance of European Public Goods: Towards a Republican Paradigm of European Integration*, Springer International Publishing, available at https://doi.org/10.1007/978-3-319-64012-9_2

Bizien, A., C. Calipel and T. Pellerin-Carlin (2024) *European Climate Investment Deficit Report: An Investment Pathway for Europe's Future*, I4CE Institute for Climate Economics, available at https://www.i4ce.org/en/publication/european-climate-investment-deficit-report-investment-pathway-europe-future/

Bolton, P., O. Edenhofer, A. Kleinnijenhuis, J. Rockström and J. Zettelmeyer (2025) 'Why coalitions of wealthy nations should fund others to decarbonize', *Nature Comment*, 13 March, available at https://www.nature.com/articles/d41586-025-00779-9

Boudbdallah, O., E. Dorrucci and C. Nerlich (2024) 'Mind the gap: Europe's strategic investment needs and how to support them', *The ECB Blog*, 27 June, European Central Bank, available at https://www.ecb.europa.eu/press/blog/date/2024/html/ecb.blog240627~2e939aa430.en.html

Brøgger, T.E. (2024) 'A "Europe of defence"? The establishment of binding commitments and supranational governance in European security and defence', *Journal of European Integration* 47(3): 403–22, available at https://doi.org/10.1080/07036337.2024.2379421

Burilkov, A. and G. Wolff (2025) 'Defending Europe without the US: first estimates of what is needed', *Analysis*, 21 February, Bruegel, available at https://www.bruegel.org/analysis/defending-europe-without-us-first-estimates-what-needed

Buti, M., A. Coloccia and M. Messori (2023) 'European public goods', *VoxEU*, 9 June, available at https://cepr.org/voxeu/columns/european-public-goods

Buti, M. and G. Papaconstantinou (2022) 'European Public Goods: How can we supply more?' *Policy Brief* 3, Luiss School of European Political Economy, available at https://leap.luiss.it/wp-content/uploads/2022/06/PB3.22-European-Public-Goods.-How-can-we-supply-more.pdf

Buti, M., Z. Darvas and A. Steinbach (2024) 'Memo to the commissioner responsible for the European Union budget', in M. Demertzis, A. Sapir and J. Zettelmeyer (eds) *Unite, defend, grow: Memos to the European Union leadership 2024-2029*, Bruegel, available at https://www.bruegel.org/memo/memo-commissioner-responsible-european-union-budget

Campos, N.F., F. Coricelli and L. Moretti (2019) 'Institutional integration and economic growth in Europe', *Journal of Monetary Economics* 103: 88–104, available at https://doi.org/10.1016/j.jmoneco.2018.08.001

CIP (2025) *Powering the future - a vision for Europe's energy system in 2050*, Copenhagen Infrastructure Partners, available at https://www.cip.com/media/nwpbhoty/powering-the-future-a-vision-for-europes-energy-system-in-2050_booklet_210x297mm_2025_spread_lowres.pdf

Claeys, G. and A. Steinbach (2024) 'A conceptual framework for the identification and governance of European public goods', *Working Paper* 14/2024, Bruegel, available at https://www.bruegel.org/working-paper/conceptual-framework-identification-and-governance-european-public-goods

Coutts, S. (2017) 'Supranational public wrongs: The limitations and possibilities of European criminal law and a European community', *Common Market Law Review* 54(3): 771-803, available at https://doi.org/10.54648/cola2017060

Crucitti, F., N.-J. Lazarou, P. Monfort and S. Salotti (2023) 'Where does the EU cohesion policy produce its benefits? A model analysis of the international spillovers generated by the policy', *Economic Systems* 47(3): 101076, available at https://doi.org/10.1016/j.ecosys.2023.101076

Darvas, Z. (2019a) 'Memo to the commissioner responsible for the European Union budget', in M. Demertzis and G.B. Wolff (eds) *Braver, greener, fairer: Memos to the EU leadership 2019-2024*, Bruegel, available at: https://www.bruegel.org/book/braver-greener-fairer-memos-eu-leadership-2019-2024

Darvas, Z. (2019b) 'Who pays for the EU budget rebates and why?' *Bruegel Blog*, 4 December, available at https://www.bruegel.org/blog-post/who-pays-eu-budget-rebates-and-why

Darvas, Z. (2020) 'Will European Union countries be able to absorb and spend well the bloc's recovery funding?' *Bruegel Blog*, 24 September, available at https://www.bruegel.org/blog-post/will-european-union-countries-be-able-absorb-and-spend-well-blocs-recovery-funding

Darvas, Z. (2022) 'The puzzle of European Union recovery plan assessments', *Bruegel Blog*, 8 February, available at https://www.bruegel.org/blog-post/puzzle-european-union-recovery-plan-assessments

Darvas, Z. and L. Welslau (2023) *First lessons from the Recovery and Resilience Facility for the EU economic governance framework*, in-depth analysis requested by the ECON Committee, European Parliament, available at https://www.bruegel.org/report/first-lessons-recovery-and-resilience-facility-eu-economic-governance-framework

Darvas, Z. and G.B. Wolff (2023) 'A Green Fiscal Pact for the EU: increasing climate investments while consolidating budgets', *Climate Policy* 23(4): 409–17, available at https://doi.org/10.1080/14693062.2022.2147893

Darvas, Z. and K. Sekut (2025) 'Greening the EU budget: why climate mainstreaming needs reform', *Analysis*, 26 February, Bruegel, available at https://www.bruegel.org/analysis/greening-eu-budget-why-climate-mainstreaming-needs-reform

Darvas, Z., L. Welslau and J. Zettelmeyer (2023) 'The EU Recovery and Resilience Facility falls short against performance-based funding standards', *Analysis*, 6 April, Bruegel, available at https://www.bruegel.org/analysis/eu-recovery-and-resilience-facility-falls-short-against-performance-based-funding

Darvas, Z., M. Dabrowski, H. Grabbe, L. Léry Moffat, A. Sapir and G. Zachmann (2024) *The impact on the European Union of Ukraine's potential future accession*, Report 02/24, Bruegel, available at https://www.bruegel.org/report/impact-european-union-ukraines-potential-future-accession

Darvas, Z. and C. McCaffrey (2024) 'Management of debt liabilities in the EU budget under the post-2027 Multiannual Financial Framework', *Briefing*, European Parliament Committee on Budgets, available at https://www.europarl.europa.eu/cmsdata/290726/5.%20Darvas%20-%20final.pdf

Darvas, Z. and J. Mejino-López (2024) 'What enlargement could imply for the European Union's budget', *Analysis*, 12 December, Bruegel, available at: https://www.bruegel.org/analysis/what-enlargement-could-imply-european-unions-budget

Demertzis, M., D. Pinkus and N. Ruer (2024) *Accelerating Strategic Investment in the European Union beyond 2026*, Report 01/24, Bruegel, available at https://www.bruegel.org/report/accelerating-strategic-investment-european-union-beyond-2026

Dustmann, C., T. Frattini and C. Halls (2010) 'Assessing the Fiscal Costs and Benefits of A8 Migration to the UK', *Fiscal Studies* 31(1): 1–41, available at https://doi.org/10.1111/j.1475-5890.2010.00106.x

ECA (2005) 'Opinion No 4/2005 on a proposal for a Council Decision on the system of the European Communities' own resources and on a proposal for a Council Regulation on the implementing measures for the correction of budgetary imbalances in accordance with Articles 4 and 5 of the Council Decision of (...) on the system of the European Communities' own resources', European Court of Auditors, available at https://eur-lex.europa.eu/legal-content/EN/ALL/?uri=CELEX:52005AA0004

ECA (2006) 'Opinion No 2/2006 on a proposal for a Council Decision on the system of the European Communities' own resources', European Court of Auditors, available at https://eur-lex.europa.eu/legal-content/EN/ALL/?uri=CELEX:52006AA0002

ECA (2012) 'Opinion No 2/2012 on an amended proposal for a Council Decision on the system of own resources of the European Union [and four other proposals]', European Court of Auditors, available at https://eur-lex.europa.eu/legal-content/EN/ALL/?uri=CELEX:52012AA0002

ECA (2021) 'Performance-based financing in Cohesion Policy: Worthy ambitions, but obstacles remained in the 2014–2020 period', *Special Report 24/2021*, European Court of Auditors, available at http://www.eca.europa.eu/en/publications/sr21_24

ECA (2023) *The Recovery and Resilience Facility's performance monitoring framework*, Special Report 26/2023, European Court of Auditors, available at https://www.eca.europa.eu/en/publications?ref=sr-2023-26

ECA (2024a) *Common Agricultural Plans: Greener, but not matching the EU's ambitions for the climate and the environment*, Special Report 20/2024, European Court of Auditors, available at https://www.eca.europa.eu/ECAPublications/SR-2024-20/SR-2024-20_EN.pdf.

ECA (2024b) *Green transition – Unclear contribution from the Recovery and Resilience Facility*, Special Report 14/2024, European Court of Auditors, available at http://www.eca.europa.eu/en/publications/sr-2024-14.

ECA (2024c) *Absorption of funds from the Recovery and Resilience Facility*, Special Report 13/2024, European Court of Auditors, available at https://www.eca.europa.eu/en/publications/sr-2024-13.

ECA (2025) 'Making the EU Electricity Grid Fit for Net-Zero Emissions', *Review* 01/2025, European Court of Auditors, available at http://www.eca.europa.eu/en/publications/rv-2025-01

ECA (2025a) *Support from the Recovery and Resilience Facility for the digital transition in EU Member States*, Special Report 13/2025, European Court of Auditors, available at https://www.eca.europa.eu/en/publications/SR-2025-13.

ECA (2025b) 'Performance-orientation, accountability and transparency – lessons to be learned from the weaknesses of the RRF,' *Review* 02/2025, European Court of Auditors, available at https://www.eca.europa.eu/en/publications/RV-2025-02

ENTSO-E (2025) *TYNDP 2024 Opportunities for a More Efficient European Power System by 2050: Infrastructure Gaps Report*, European Network of Transmission System Operators for Electricity, available at https://www.entsoe.eu/outlooks/tyndp/2024/#reports

European Commission (2017) *EU Budget Focused on Results*, Summary of the 1st annual conference held on 22 September, 2015, De Gasperi Hall, European Commission, Brussels, available at https://op.europa.eu/en/publication-detail/-/publication/368788bd-45ad-11e7-aea8-01aa75ed71a1

European Commission (2020a) *Supporting the Implementation of CEF2 Digital*, Final Report, available at https://op.europa.eu/en/publication-detail/-/publication/8947e9db-4eda-11ea-aece-01aa75ed71a1/language-en

European Commission (2020b) 'Europe's moment: Repair and Prepare for the Next Generation,' SWD/2020/98 final, available at: https://eur-lex.europa.eu/legal-content/EN/TXT/?uri=celex:52020SC0098

European Commission (2021a) 'The evolving nature of the EU budget,' *EU Budget Policy Brief* 1, Directorate-General for Budget, available at www.doi.org/10.2761/216223

European Commission (2021b) 'Proposal for a Council Decision amending Decision (EU, Euratom) 2020/2053 on the system of own resources of the European Union,' COM/2021/570 final, https://eur-lex.europa.eu/legal-content/EN/TXT/?uri=CELEX%3A52021PC0570

European Commission (2021c) *The EU's 2021-2027 long-term budget and NextGenerationEU: Facts and figures*, Directorate-General for Budget, available at https://data.europa.eu/doi/10.2761/808559

European Commission (2022) 'Towards a green, digital and resilient economy: our European Growth Model,' COM(2022) 83 final, available at https://eur-lex.europa.eu/legal-content/EN/TXT/?uri=CELEX%3A52022DC0083

European Commission (2022a) 'Proposal for a Regulation on establishing the European defence industry Reinforcement through common Procurement Act,' COM(2022) 349 final, available at https://eur-lex.europa.eu/legal-content/EN/TXT/?uri=celex:52022PC0349

European Commission (2023a) 'Investment needs assessment and funding availabilities to strengthen EU's Net-Zero technology manufacturing capacity', SWD(2023) 68, available at https://single-market-economy.ec.europa.eu/publications/staff-working-document-investment-needs-assessment-and-funding-availabilities-strengthen-eus-net_en

European Commission (2023b) 'An adjusted package for the next generation of own resources', COM(2023) 330 final, available at https://commission.europa.eu/system/files/2023-06/COM_2023_330_1_EN_ACT_part1_v5.pdf

European Commission (2023c) 'Proposal for a Council Directive on Business in Europe: Framework for Income Taxation (BEFIT)', COM/2023/532 final, available at https://eur-lex.europa.eu/legal-content/EN/

European Commission (2024) 'Impact Assessment, Securing our future - Europe's 2040 climate target and path to climate neutrality by 2050 building a sustainable, just and prosperous society', SWD(2024) 63 final, available at https://eur-lex.europa.eu/legal-content/EN/TXT/?uri=CELEX%3A52024SC0063

European Parliament (2023) 'European Parliament resolution of 10 May 2023 on own resources: a new start for EU finances, a new start for Europe', 2022/2172(INI), available at https://www.europarl.europa.eu/doceo/document/TA-9-2023-0195_EN.html

Expert Group for a Green Tax Reform (2024) *Green Tax Reform – Final Report*, available at https://skm.dk/media/tngh1b4r/green-tax-reform-final-report.pdf

Felbermayr, G. and A. Pekanov (2024) *Pan-European Public Goods: Rationale, Financing and Governance*, Study requested by the ECON Committee, European Parliament, available at https://www.europarl.europa.eu/thinktank/de/document/IPOL_STU(2024)755726

Fiore, A. and H. Grabbe (2025), 'Nature markets: how can credits and shares provide durable, additional finance?', *Policy Brief* 20/2025, Bruegel, available at https://www.bruegel.org/policy-brief/nature-markets-how-can-credits-and-shares-provide-durable-additional-finance

Fuest, C. and J. Pisani-Ferry (2019) *A Primer on Developing European Public Goods*, EconPol Policy Report, available at https://www.econstor.eu/handle/10419/219519

García Antón, R. and A. Lejour (2023) 'The Justification, Design and Revenues of a Single Market Levy', *Policy Brief*, Socialists & Democrats Group in the European Parliament, available at https://www.socialistsanddemocrats.eu/sites/default/files/2023-12/the_justification_design_and_revenues_of_a_single_market_levy_231205.pdf

GFCC (2009) 'Judgment of the Second Senate of 30 June 2009 (2 BvE 2/08)', German Federal Constitutional Court, available at https://www.bundesverfassungsgericht.de/SharedDocs/Entscheidungen/EN/2009/06/es20090630_2bve000208en.html

Grabbe, H. and L. Léry Moffat (2024) 'A European circular single market for economic security and competitiveness', *Policy Brief* 20/2024, Bruegel, available at https://www.bruegel.org/policy-brief/european-circular-single-market-economic-security-and-competitiveness

Graichen, J. and S. Ludig (2024) *Supply and demand in the ETS 2. Assessment of the new EU ETS for road transport, buildings and other sectors*, Climate Change 09/2024, German Environment Agency, available at https://www.umweltbundesamt.de/publikationen/supply-demand-in-the-ets-2

Grund, S. and A. Steinbach (2023) 'European Union debt financing: leeway and barriers from a legal perspective', *Working Paper* 15/2023, Bruegel, available at https://www.bruegel.org/working-paper/european-union-debt-financing-leeway-and-barriers-legal-perspective

Guyomard H., M. Stickel, C. Détang-Dessendre, L.-G. Soler, P.-M. Aubert, A. Carpentier ... S. Thoyer (2024), *Research for AGRI Committee – The next reform of the CAP: The variables in the equation*, Study requested by the AGRI Committee, European Parliament, available at https://www.europarl.europa.eu/thinktank/en/document/CASP_STU(2025)759316

Heussaff, C. and G. Zachmann (2025) 'Upgrading Europe's electricity grid is about more than just money', *Policy Brief* 04/2025, Bruegel, available at https://www.bruegel.org/policy-brief/upgrading-europes-electricity-grid-about-more-just-money

IMF (2024) *Regional Economic Outlook, Europe, October 2024*, International Monetary Fund, available at https://www.elibrary.imf.org/display/book/9798400287312/9798400287312.xml

Jüngling, E., G. Sgaravatti, S. Tagliapietra and G. Zachmann (2025) 'Making the best of the new EU Social and Climate Fund', *Policy Brief* 14/2025, Bruegel, available at https://www.bruegel.org/policy-brief/making-best-new-eu-social-climate-fund

Keen, M. and J. Strand (2007) 'Indirect taxes on international aviation', *Fiscal Studies* 28(1): 1-41, available at https://doi.org/10.1111/j.1475-5890.2007.00046.x

Keliauskaite, U., B. McWilliams, G. Sgaravatti and S. Tagliapietra (2025) 'Financing European Union's buildings' decarbonisation strategy', *Energy Policy* 198: 114437, available at https://doi.org/10.1016/j.enpol.2024.114437

Kengyel, Á. (2022) 'Would Renationalisation and Co-financing of the Common Agricultural Policy Be Justified?' *Intereconomics* 57(2): 113–19, available at https://doi.org/10.1007/s10272-022-1038-5

Kribbe, H. and L. van Middelaar (2023) 'Preparing for the next EU enlargement: Tough choices ahead,' *BIG002*, Brussels Institute for Geopolitics, available at https://big-europe.eu/publications/big002-preparing-for-the-next-eu-enlargement

Kubelovká, V., M. Sanz, L. Schmoigl, M. Schratzenstaller, A. Sutrich and P. Heimberger (2024) *Mapping the current structure and discovering the potential of 'other revenue'*, Study requested by the BUDG Committee, European Parliament, available at https://www.europarl.europa.eu/thinktank/en/document/BUDG_STU(2025)768313

Landau, J.-P. (2004) *Les Nouvelles contribution financières internationales*, Report for the French Presidency, available at https://www.vie-publique.fr/rapport/26622-les-nouvelles-contributions-financieres-internationales

Lilyanova, V. (2021) 'Neighbourhood and the World, Heading 6 of the 2021-2027 MFF,' *Briefing*, European Parliamentary Research Service, available at https://www.europarl.europa.eu/RegData/etudes/BRIE/2021/690546/EPRS_BRI(2021)690546_EN.pdf

Martens, B. (2024) 'An institutional economics approach to data spaces as data market intermediaries,' mimeo, available at https://doi.org/10.2139/ssrn.4731126

M'barek, R., J. Barreiro Hurle, P. Boulanger, A. Caivano, P. Ciaian, H. Dudu ... G. Genovese, *Scenar 2030 - Pathways for the European agriculture and food sector beyond 2020*, Summary Report, Joint Research Centre, European Commission, available at https://publications.jrc.ec.europa.eu/repository/handle/JRC109053

Medve-Bálint, G. (2014) 'The Role of the EU in Shaping FDI Flows to East Central Europe,' *Journal of Common Market Studies* 52: 35-51, available at https://doi.org/10.1111/jcms.12077

Monti, M., D. Dăianu, C. Fuest, K. Georgieva, I. Kalfin, A. Lamassoure, P. Moscovici, I. Šimonytė, F. Timmermans and G. Verhofstadt (2017) *Future financing of the EU*, Final report and recommendations of the High Level Group on Own Resources December 2016, available at https://commission.europa.eu/strategy-and-policy/eu-budget/long-term-eu-budget/2014-2020/revenue/high-level-group-own-resources_en

Moynihan, D. and I. Beazley (2016) *Toward Next-Generation Performance Budgeting: Lessons from the Experiences of Seven Reforming Countries*, World Bank Group, available at https://documents1.worldbank.org/curated/en/356081478497402740/pdf/109808-PUB-Box396311B-PUBLIC-DOCDATE-11-1-16.pdf

Mueller, T. (2024) 'Drivers and Impact of European Defence Market Integration: A Literature Meta-Synthesis with Economic Focus,' *Defence and Peace Economics*, 1–36, available at https://doi.org/10.1080/10242694.2024.2396416

Oates, W. (1972) *Fiscal Federalism*, Harcourt Brace Jovanovich

OECD (2007) *Performance Budgeting in OECD Countries*, Organisation for Economic Co-operation and Development, available at https://doi.org/10.1787/9789264034051-en

OECD (2013) 'Addressing Base Erosion and Profit Shifting,' Organisation for Economic Co-operation and Development, available at https://doi.org/10.1787/9789264192744-en

Ostanina, S. (2024) 'Turbo-charging the EU's defence industry and security posture,' *Policy Brief*, Jacques Delors Centre, Hertie School, available at https://www.delorscentre.eu/en/publications/detail/publication/turbo-charging-the-eus-defence-industry-and-security-posture

Paine, J. (2018) 'International Adjudication as a Global Public Good?' *European Journal of International Law*, 29(4): 1223–49, available at https://doi.org/10.1093/ejil/chy075

Pe'er, G., J.A. Finn, M. Díaz, M. Birkenstock, S. Lakner, N. Röder ... H. Guyomard (2022) 'How can the European Common Agricultural Policy help halt biodiversity loss? Recommendations by over 300 experts,' *Conservation Letters* 15(6), available at https://doi.org/10.1111/conl.12901

Pe'er, G., S. Lakner, R. Müller, G. Passoni, V. Bontzorlos, D. Clough ... Y. Zinngrebe (2017) *Is the CAP Fit for purpose? An evidence-based fitness check assessment*, German Centre for Integrative Biodiversity Research (iDiv) Jena-Halle-Leipzig, available at https://idiv-biodiversity.de/fileadmin/content/iDiv_Files/Documents/executive_summary_17.11_final.pdf

Pisani-Ferry, J. and S. Tagliapietra (2024) 'An investment strategy to keep the European Green Deal on track,' *Policy Brief* 31/2024, Bruegel, available at https://www.bruegel.org/policy-brief/investment-strategy-keep-european-green-deal-track

PwC (2024) *Market Failure and Barriers to Investment*, Irish Department of the Environment, Climate and Communications, available at https://www.gov.ie/en/consultation/80439-consultation-on-international-connectivity-for-telecommunications/

Roth, A. and W.-P. Schill (2023) 'Geographical balancing of wind power decreases storage needs in a 100% renewable European power sector', *iScience* 26(7), available at https://doi.org/10.1016/j.isci.2023.107074

Rubio, E., C. Alcidi, R. Hansum, T. Akhvlediani, I. Begg, J. Lindler and B. Couteau (2025) *Adapting the EU budget to make it fit for the purpose of future enlargements*, Study requested by the BUDG Committee, European Parliament, available at https://www.europarl.europa.eu/thinktank/en/document/BUDG_STU(2025)769193

Saint-Amans, P. (2024) 'Broader border taxes: a new option for European Union budget resources', *Policy Brief* 06/2024, Bruegel, available at https://www.bruegel.org/policy-brief/broader-border-taxes-new-option-european-union-budget-resources

Samuelson, P.A. (1954) 'The Pure Theory of Public Expenditure', *The Review of Economics and Statistics* 36(4), available at https://www.jstor.org/stable/1925895

Saulnier, J., A. Heflich, L. Jančová, I.-M. Florea and K. Grosse Kohorst (2025) 'Benefit of an EU strategic innovation agenda', *Briefing*, European Parliamentary Research Service, available at https://www.europarl.europa.eu/RegData/etudes/STUD/2025/762853/EPRS_STU(2025)762853_EN.pdf

Schout, A. (2024) *Cohesion Policy: A Management Audit*, Clingendael Report, Netherlands Institute of International Relations, available at https://www.clingendael.org/publication/cohesion-policy-management-audit

Spicker, P. (2024) 'The effect of treating public services as commodities', *Public Money & Management* 44(4): 281–88, available at https://doi.org/10.1080/09540962.2023.2240641

Steinbach, A. (2025) *EU Law and Economics*, Oxford University Press

Thöne, M. (2024) 'European Public Goods and the 2028-2034 Multiannual Financial Framework: Financing the EU in a decade of reform', *Briefing* requested by the BUDG Committee, European Parliament, available at https://www.europarl.europa.eu/cmsdata/290937/3.%20Thoene%20-%20final2.pdf

Tibor, D. (2020) 'EU Added Value—a Categorical Imperative for EU Action?', *Journal* 3/2020, European Court of Auditors, available at https://www.eca.europa.eu/Lists/ECADocuments/JOURNAL20_03/JOURNAL20_03.pdf

Tiebout, C.M. (1956) 'A Pure Theory of Local Expenditures', *Journal of Political Economy* 64(5), available at https://www.journals.uchicago.edu/doi/abs/10.1086/257839

Trachtman, J. (2000) 'Regulatory competition and regulatory jurisdiction', *Journal of International Economic Law* 3(2): 331–48, available at https://doi.org/10.1093/jiel/3.2.331

WIK-Consult (2023) *Investment and Funding Needs for the Digital Decade Connectivity Targets*, study for the European Commission, available at https://ec.europa.eu/newsroom/dae/redirection/document/97376

Wolff, G., A. Steinbach and J. Zettelmeyer (2025) 'The governance and funding of European rearmament', *Policy Brief* 15/2025, Bruegel, available at https://www.bruegel.org/policy-brief/governance-and-funding-european-rearmament

WWF (2024) 'Can your money do better? Redirecting harmful subsidies to foster nature & climate resilience', WWF European Policy Office, available at https://wwfeu.awsassets.panda.org/downloads/wwf---harmful-subsidies-report_full-report.pdf

Wyplosz, C. (2024) *Which European Public Goods?* In-Depth Analysis requested by the ECON Committee, European Parliament, available at https://www.europarl.europa.eu/RegData/etudes/IDAN/2024/755722/IPOL_IDA(2024)755722_EN.pdf

Zeitlin, J., D. Bokhorst and E. Eihmanis (2023) *Rethinking the Governance and Delivery of the Cohesion Policy Funds: Is the Recovery and Resilience Facility (RRF) a Model?* Expert paper prepared for High-Level Group on the Future of Cohesion Policy, European Commission, available at https://hdl.handle.net/1814/76078

Zettelmeyer, J., A. Steinbach and G. Wolff (2025) 'The proposed European Defence Mechanism: questions and answers', *Analysis*, 16 April, Bruegel, available at https://www.bruegel.org/analysis/proposed-european-defence-mechanism-questions-and-answers

Annex 1: The MFF's seven main headings and their EPG relevance

This annex provides a programme-by-programme analysis of EU spending items under each 2021-2027 MFF heading to identify what spending can be classed as spending on European public goods. See chapter 2, section 2.3 for a summary analysis, and Figure 1 in chapter 2 for a summary by heading.

A1.1 Heading 1: Single market, innovation and digital (€150 billion)

Heading 1 – single market, innovation and digital – covers spending in four policy areas: research and innovation, European strategic investments, single market and space. The heading currently has €150 billion allocated to it (European Commission, 2021c), or about 12 percent of the total EU budget. Most of this heading can be classified as EPGs. The heading includes minor spending on non-public goods and national public goods. We look at each of the four policy areas in turn.

A1.1.1 Research and innovation

Horizon Europe (€90 billion)

Horizon Europe is the EU's main research and innovation funding programme. Knowledge is a classical (global) public good. Freely available, non-rival in consumption, it creates positive spillovers and is subject to economies of scale (Wyplosz, 2024). While research in the EU is done predominantly at national level, largely through a wide range of institutions such as universities and research centres, there is a strong rationale for European research to facilitate knowledge-sharing. A European Research Area provides economies of scale and internalises positive externalities from research.

In terms of economies of scale, significant benefits can be unlocked in areas where national research would otherwise not happen. Examples include cost-intensive research, which often requires a sufficiently high level of investment to be successful. Certain risk-prone and expensive research projects (such as the EU satellite navigation system Galileo) benefit from sharing of the investment across multiple parties (Tibor, 2020). The European Innovation Council, part of the Horizon programme, is illustrative in this regard. It supports potential breakthrough innovation with scale-up potential but which may be too risky for private investors to support. In many other cases, avoiding duplication is an argument for centralising and coordinating research activities. Horizon Europe can thus be fully categorised as an EPG.

Euratom research and training programme (€2 billion)

Similar considerations apply to the Euratom research and training programme. By providing nuclear research and training in the EU, the programme enables an EU-wide approach to nuclear safety and security. It also enhances emergency preparedness in case of a nuclear accident (which would have cross-border impact) and funds the Joint Research Centre's nuclear-related activities, such as provision of independent scientific advice in the field of nuclear safety. With the civil use of nuclear technology being of interest to all EU members, there is a rationale for centralising Euratom research and training at EU level, for knowledge-sharing and to take advantage of economies of scale. We thus categorise Euratom fully as an EPG.

International Thermonuclear Experimental Reactor (ITER) (€6 billion)

Likewise, the International Thermonuclear Experimental Reactor (ITER) project, which supports the construction of the reactor with the long-term objective of exploiting nuclear fusion, can be considered an

EPG. If EU countries pursued this kind of research individually, it would likely be under-funded and would waste resources through duplication of research. ITER supports the creation and better sharing of excellent knowledge and technologies, and thus falls under the EPG category.

A1.1.2 European strategic investments

InvestEU Fund (€4 billion)

The InvestEU Programme is one of the EU's investment support mechanisms, bringing various financial instruments within a single structure. It contains a fund intended to mobilise private investment for the EU's top policy priorities, such as the green and digital transitions, innovation and social investments and skills.

InvestEU is designed to counterbalance market failures (Regulation (EU) 2021/523, Article 8(1)) and to deliver public goods (Regulation (EU) 2021/523, Annex V). In relation to market failures, InvestEU offers multiple financing programmes, including with the European Investment Bank (EIB), intended to crowd-in private investors and provide sufficient risk diversification. With co-financing by the EU and EU countries, there is no risk that the task of addressing market failure will be shifted to one level only. In principle, InvestEU's focus on de-risking investment qualifies it as spending on a public good. However, this is only the case if the underlying good being financed can be classified as a public good.

The question is thus whether the InvestEU fund delivers private goods, NPGs or EPGs. Its funding of sustainable infrastructure (without including cross-border requirements) can be classified as spending on a public good with national character. While it does not explicitly exclude cross-border projects, we assume such projects to be mostly national, given that the Connection Europe Facility (see below) specifically addresses this. The second policy area covers research, innovation and digitalisation, focusing on product development and the scaling-up of innovative companies without sector specification. Given that the scaling up of innovative sectors does not necessarily imply the provision of public goods, we assume that this focuses on private goods, while acknowledging that some public goods might be funded under this policy area as well. Similar considerations apply to support for SMEs. Social investment and skills can be classified as private goods as argued further below (see the section on the Digital Europe Programme). InvestEU's focus thus appears limited to the pursuit of NPGs and private goods.

Connecting Europe Facility (CEF, €21 billion)

Construction and operation of essential facilities including electricity, digital networks and railways are considered private goods given their excludability. A rationale for public funding exists only in relation to crowding-in, where private investment would otherwise not take place. The Facility furthers development of the Trans-European Transport Network (TEN-T), focusing on missing links and cross-border projects with an EU added value. Both CEF Energy (€6 billion) and CEF Transport (€13 billion) follow a genuine externality logic by focusing on funding programmes that promote cross-border energy and transport infrastructure. EU countries alone do not account for the positive externality that cross-border movement of goods and persons (transport) and cross-border flow of electricity and gas (energy) have for other EU countries. Both CEF Energy and CEF Transport can thus be classified as EPGs.

CEF Digital (€2 billion) follows the same reasoning to the extent that the Facility funds cross-border digital infrastructure. This programme expands 5G systems along all major transport paths, including the trans-European transport networks, and creates capacity for cross-border connectivity when market failure occurs (European Commission, 2020) and national public funding is insufficient. There are strong pan-European aspects, for instance, to the backbone connectivity for Digital Global Gateways that secure networks that transport large volumes of data across long distances, such as submarine cables and satellite links, for which market failure persists because of private underinvestment (PwC, 2024). CEF Digital can thus also be considered as investing in EPGs.

Digital Europe Programme (DEP, €8 billion)

The EPG character of the Digital Europe programme is less obvious. Dedicated to the digital transformation of public services and businesses through high-performance computing, it focuses on artificial intelligence, digital skills and cybersecurity. However, the digital transition is not a public good, but rather a private good that should be funded privately (Wyplosz, 2024). Digitisation and digitalisation of the economy are primarily driven and funded by corporations seeking a competitive edge, making digital products private and competitive products. A rationale for public funding exists only in cases of crowding-in, when private investment would not occur otherwise, or for the provision of research. Whether this applies must be assessed in relation to each policy objective of the Digital Europe Programme (Article 8 of Regulation (EU) 2021/694).

The DEP pursues six different specific objectives, each leading to a different EPG assessment (Article 3(2) of Regulation (EU) 2021/694). The first objective, supercomputing, is promoted by the EU to pursue a leading role in the digital economy, but there is no compelling case to consider high-performance computing as an EPG, as it relates solely to digitalisation, a private good. The relevant regulation sets the goal *"to develop, deploy, extend and maintain in the Union an integrated world-class supercomputing and data infrastructure"* (Article 3(1) of Regulation (EU) 2018/1488). Thus, it does not include a pure research element that would justify classification as an EPG on an economy-of-scale and positive externality basis (see discussion of research funds). We thus categorise spending allocated to this objective of the DEP as a private good (25 percent of DEP spending).

The second DEP objective, artificial intelligence, is pursued in connection with supercomputing, aiming to *"build up and strengthen core AI capacities and knowledge in the Union, including building up and strengthening quality data resources"* (Article 5 of Regulation (EU) 2021/694). Yet, the funding does not focus on market failures that warrant EU intervention, with no clear focus on programmes that would be sidelined if AI were funded at national level in line with national priorities. The default assumption is that AI technologies are private goods, with only market failure justifying state intervention. Further, there is no explicit requirement for economies of scale or EU added value, which makes this programme more appropriate for the national level (private or public). We thus classify this objective as a private good (20 percent of DEP spending).

Objective 3 of the DEP – digital security, and cybersecurity in particular – is a transnational public good. Externalities and economies of scale are present in both data protection and cybersecurity, which are European public goods because preferences for this good are assumed to be consistent across the EU, and national authorities lack information that would lead to more efficient implementation at national level (Wyplosz, 2024). With cybersecurity characterised as a public good in which the level of vulnerability is determined by the weakest link, there is rationale for achieving a *"high common level of cybersecurity at European level"* (Article 6(1a) of Regulation (EU) 2021/694) and we thus classify funding under this objective as spending on EPGs (17 percent of DEP spending).

Developing advanced digital skills (DEP Objective 4) to improve Europe's talent pool is an unconvincing EPG. While basic and primary education is a public good best delivered at national level (Wyplosz, 2024), the reskilling of workers and continuous learning is more adequately characterised as a private good, supplied by the private sector (6 percent of DEP spending).

The deployment and best use of digital capacities and interoperability goal (DEP Objective 5) aims at *"bridging the digital divide"*. It focuses on trans-European digital infrastructure and is intended to be *"in complementarity with national and regional actions"*, which indicates a focus on activities and infrastructures from which positive externalities can be generated through centralised action (Article 8(1) of Regulation

(EU) 2021/694). We thus categorise most spending under this objective as an EPG (11 percent of DEP spending). However, this objective also includes funding of European Digital Innovation Hubs (EDIH) (1 percent of DEP spending), which we do not consider as an EPG. The hubs offer access to technology testing and support the digital transformation of private and public organisations across Europe, including government at national, regional and local levels. Supporting companies in responding to digital challenges by providing access to technical expertise and innovation services misses two characteristics of EPGs. First, there is no compelling market failure reason why market actors could not supply these services. Second, national governments are well equipped to support private companies when needed. Without externalities or economies of scale, there is no reason why EU countries shouldn't fund these activities via their national budgets. Furthermore, EDIHs are present regionally and provide services to local companies, depending on language and the local innovation ecosystem. Their funding thus meets local needs, and EU countries, rather than the EU, should supply this. In addition, digitisation of public services – another objective of EDIHs – is a national public good that does not need to be funded by the EU.

Objective 6 (semiconductors) is driven by industrial policy concerns which cannot build on an EPG logic. This budget line does not support research. Instead, it supports *"building up advanced design capacities"*. To the extent that semiconductors are seen as a geopolitically important technology, this industrial policy preference is not a public good concern. There is no cross-border element, nor are economies of scale at the core of the budget line. Competitiveness, a driver behind the goal of promoting the semiconductor industry, is not in itself an EPG. Rather it entails and seeks to extend certain public goods, such as public services, infrastructure, taxation and judicial frameworks, which are mostly national and local (Wyplosz, 2024). We thus classify this objective as a policy preference and not a public good (19 percent of DEP spending).

A1.1.3 Single market

The single market is a European public good. Whenever EU countries make rules on the basis of national interests, but that might hinder cross-border commerce, they could inflict negative or produce positive externalities on other European states. Harmonised legislation can produce economies of scale that tap the growth potential of a common market. Yet, in order to protect variable preferences, countries should keep some leeway to deviate from rules because of core sovereign concerns (such as national security or protection of life and safety) (Steinbach, 2025).

Single Market Programme (€4 billion)

The Single Market Programme seeks to tackle single-market fragmentation and helps consumers and small and medium-sized enterprises (SMEs) to take full advantage of the single market. The Programme's specific objectives (Regulation (EU) 2021/690, Article 3) include the removal of obstacles to commerce and fostering standardisation to boost economies of scale. In addition, the objectives of protecting consumers, product safety and the health of humans and animals are dealt with on the EU level to avoid fragmentation. EU members also maintain leeway to permit deviations in justified cases, ensuring that different preferences are taken into account. Another objective on the collection of data and ensuring its free availability through statistics also offers added value across EU members. We therefore classify this programme as an EPG.

A1.1.4 Space

EU Space Programme (€15 billion)

Space activities can involve European public goods, as they make economies of scale through the pooling of resources. Investing in space infrastructure and technologies is cost-intensive in terms of research and implementation. Sharing investment across multiple parties is better when engaging in risk-prone and expensive research projects. All EU countries benefit from EU space activities such as the Galileo satellite system and the Copernicus Earth observation programme.

A1.1.5 Heading 1: summary

Figure A1 summarises the assessments in the previous sections by classification of spending. The majority of this heading is in the EPG category. This is mostly driven by the focus on research and the cross-border aspects of many of the funding allocations (eg CEF). The non-PG classification refers mostly to programmes that support the private sector in a capacity that goes beyond the provision of public goods, such as digitalisation.

Figure A1: Spending categorisation by programme, Heading 1 (%)

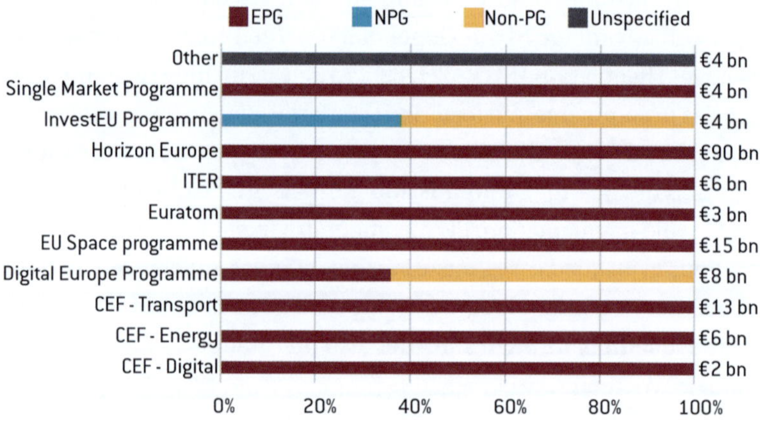

Source: Bruegel. Note: 'other' includes cooperation in the field of customs and taxation, the EU anti-fraud programme, decentralised agencies and budget items categorised as other.

A1.2 Heading 2: Cohesion, resilience and values (€427 billion)

The objective of spending under this heading is to boost resilience and cohesion between EU countries, with a focus on reducing regional disparities and promoting sustainable territorial development. The heading allows for €427 billion of spending, which makes up around 35 percent of the total EU budget, making it the largest heading. Less than half of this heading can be classified as EPGs. Most of the funding under this heading can be considered as pursuing the integration objective.

A1.2.1 Regional Development and Cohesion

European Regional Development Fund (ERDF, €226 billion)

The ERDF is meant to strengthen EU economic, social and territorial cohesion, with the specific goals of levelling up EU regions, particularly the least-favoured regions (Article 2(2) Regulation (EU) 2021/1058).

Such levelling up is however more a policy preference than a public good. Differences in the level of economic development, measured under the ERDF as *per-capita* gross national income as a share of the EU average, results from various social, historical and economic factors. Differences in regional economic strength remain pronounced, reflecting path dependencies, persistent barriers to economic convergence (eg brain drain), private choices (of business investment and labour supply in the regions concerned) and public policy choices (such as structural reforms). In the logic of fiscal competition, economic differences are productive because they lead regions to compete to offer the best conditions for workers and companies (Trachtman, 2000).

Additionally, economic disparity presents a compelling argument for negative impacts on other countries in only a few cases, including:

- Economic spillovers transmitted through demand and purchasing power;
- Increased migration from lagging regions;
- Potential gains for extreme political parties in lagging areas, making common decision-making more challenging for prosperous regions;
- Fiscal sustainability risks in lagging regions that could negatively impact prosperous regions.

However, there is no indication that economic differences across Europe will give rise to social unrest to a degree that would significantly undermine the stability of the European common market, or constitute a security threat for other EU members. Nor are economies of scale associated with economic convergence. For instance, providing ERDF funding to *"disadvantaged regions and areas, in particular rural areas and areas which suffer from severe and permanent natural or demographic handicaps"* (see Article 10, Regulation (EU) 2021/1058), is primarily a policy preference for regional redistribution. This is not to say that regions do not produce spillovers for each other (eg through the four factors listed above), and in extreme cases, there may be grounds for public-good intervention (eg to sustain currency stability). However, an imbalance in *per-capita* economic strength can be the result of market-based adjustment processes. Addressing those can be a legitimate policy objective, but it is not a public good remedy (Begg, 2008).

In some cases, ERDF expenditure may contribute to European public goods, such as when investment in infrastructure incidentally has cross-border implications, or when the fund contributes to environmental protection (Article 5(1) (a) and (b) of Regulation (EU) 2021/1058).

Rather, economic convergence has always been a priority for European integration, as stipulated in the European Treaties. Redistribution from richer to poorer regions is a policy preference, which requires coordination at the EU level if the redistribution is to occur evenly across EU countries. They should thus be classified as policy preferences favouring EU integration but they do not pursue European public goods, nor are they national public goods, notwithstanding their strong anchor in the European Treaties. Therefore, only EDRF spending on sustainability and infrastructure can be considered spending on EPGs. This makes up about 44 percent of spending.

Cohesion Fund (€48 billion)

The Cohesion Fund is targeted at EU countries with GNI *per capita* below 90 percent of the EU average. It shares the ERDF objectives of reducing regional disparities and economic divergence. However, unlike the ERDF, the Cohesion Fund concentrates its funding on the environment, climate action and trans-European transport networks and infrastructure. These expenditure targets have an EPG character. Investment in environmental improvement and climate action contribute to the protection of a global public good, and these centralised investments create positive externalities that national funding would not be able to deliver. Also, cross-border infrastructure makes national infrastructure expenditure more effective and thereby represents a positive externality, which creates a rationale for Europe-wide funding. Thus, unlike the ERDF, most of the Cohesion Fund can be considered as targeting an EPG.

EU4Health Programme (€6 billion)

Most healthcare is delivered locally according to a wide variety of long-standing institutional arrangements and in line with national and regional preferences. There are returns to scale, but they diminish quickly so that most of the associated benefits can be reaped locally or nationally (Wyplosz, 2024). Health cannot be considered a fully-fledged EPG in light of significant differences in preferences.

The logic is different if externalities and economies of scale become so great that they outstrip different preferences. A pandemic is an obvious case in which externalities are so significant that coordinated EU-wide action is justified. In a pandemic, there could be major spillovers because of the risk of contagion between countries if there is insufficient prevention and/or insufficient crisis response in one country. Health then becomes a 'weakest-link' public good. This contrasts with the main health services provided at national level, which are typically characterised by national idiosyncrasies and path-dependence, and which should therefore remain in national hands. Accordingly, EU centralised power must be limited to preventing negative cross-border spillovers and to taking advantage of economies of scale (Claeys and Steinbach, 2024).

EU4Health seeks to complement national health-improvement

measures and to help ensure a high level of health protection across all EU policy areas and measures. However, based on the above mixed public-good character of health, EU4Health only partly pursues objectives for which externalities or economies of scale are significant. Reducing the burden of communicable and non-communicable diseases supports the provision of national public goods rather than qualifying as an EPG itself. Externalities from these diseases (especially from non-communicable diseases) are not large enough to justify centralised action, even less as this objective also seeks to *"foster healthy lifestyles"* (Article 3 (a) of Regulation (EU) 2021/522).

Likewise, improving the availability of medical products and medical devices as general policy (not limited to contagion-related medical goods) does not give the public good a European character. Nor does the strengthening of health systems by improving their resilience and resource efficiency respond to the cross-border nature of health. By contrast, there is a rationale for an EPG to the extent that the programme seeks to protect people from *"serious cross-border threats to health and strengthening the responsiveness of health systems and coordination among the EU members in order to cope with serious cross-border threats to health"*. The concentration on the cross-border nature of health issues underscores the spillovers associated with threats to health, justifying this type of cross-border coordination as an EPG.

The efforts described above can be assigned to different clusters under the fund. Crisis preparedness, which, for example, includes the prevention of cross-border threats to health, can be considered an EPG. Other clusters, such as prevention and improving the availability of medical services, as argued above, can be categorised as NPGs[51].

51 We categorise spending allocated to the different clusters based on the reported spending in work programmes for 2021 to 2024.

A1.2.2 Investing in people, social cohesion and values

European Social Fund + (ESF+, €99 billion)

Social policies are deeply rooted in national cultures and historical path-dependencies. While preferences vary significantly, externalities and economies of scale are limited. There may be an exception to this if social policies constitute barriers to free movement in the internal market, for instance by deterring workers from seeking work abroad because social entitlements would be lost. Except for a limited set of occasions in which coordination of the social policies of EU countries is necessary (eg transfer of social claims), EU social spending constitutes a policy preference and not a public good.

The objectives of ESF+ go well beyond what a public-good concept would suggest (Regulation (EU) 2021/1057, Article 3). Supporting EU countries and regions to achieve high employment levels, fair social protection and a skilled and resilient workforce are policy preferences that can be pursued better in line with national and regional preferences. Similarly, ensuring equal opportunities and access to the labour market, fair and high-quality working conditions and inclusive education and training are laudable policy objectives that may generally lead to a functioning labour market. However, there is no compelling reason why such goals must be set at European level rather than in alignment with regional and local preferences. There is no indication that the ESF+ tackles cross-border issues of social policy in particular. The ESF+ should therefore, like cohesion policies, be considered as pursuing an integration objective.

Erasmus+ (€27 billion)

Education is a public good. While rival in nature, education is not sufficiently provided by markets and at the same time produces a high level of positive spillovers. However, education is provided at national level and in line with national notions of education and professional and personal development.

For education to qualify as an EPG, it requires positive cross-border externalities, similar to research. This implies that education can be considered an EPG, if the quality of education improves through exposure of students to other European education facilities.

Erasmus+ is the EU's programme to support education, training, young people and sport. The programme's general objective is to support, through lifelong learning, educational, professional and personal development of people. The programme aims to build a European Education Area, supporting the implementation of European strategic cooperation in the field of education and training (See Regulation (EU) 2021/817).

In addition to these general goals, Erasmus+ requires funding only for those actions and activities that generate European added value. This can be ensured through transnational activities (eg learning mobility) or complementarity or synergies with programmes in other states, or on an international level.

On this basis, Erasmus+ funding is limited to programmes to which national educational systems would not contribute, and to programmes that create economies of scale. Similar considerations apply to other programmes: the European Solidarity Corps and Creative Europe generate economies of scale. While cultural exchange and solidarity activities remain rooted in national policies, both of these programmes limit these activities to actions with transnational character, cross-border cooperation and economies of scale.

A1.2.3 Heading 2: summary

Figure A2 summarises the previous sections and plots the classification of spending by programme. Large parts of the spending under this heading pursue integration objectives. This is mostly driven by the ERDF and the ESF+, which serve re-distributional purposes. The EPG character of spending under this heading is mostly determined by cross-border infrastructure investment and action to mitigate climate change.

Figure A2: Heading 2, categorisation of spending by programme (%)

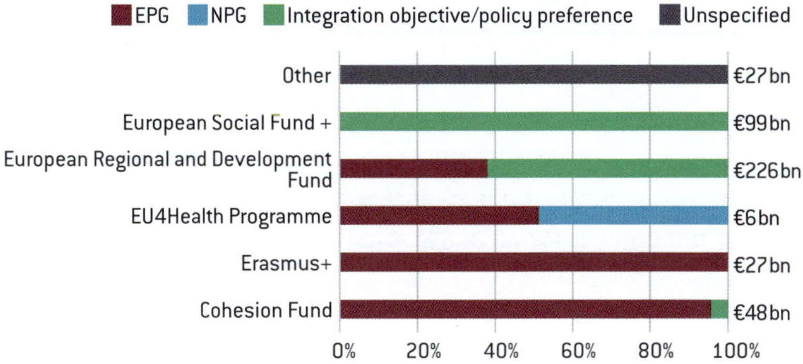

Sources: Bruegel. Note: 'other' includes Creative Europe, the European Solidarity Corps, financing and repayment of NGEU, Justice Rights and Values, Protection of the Euro Against Counterfeiting, Support to the Turkish Cypriot Community, Union Civil Protection Mechanism, decentralised agencies and budget items categorised as other.

A1.3 Heading 3: Natural Resources and Environment (€400 billion)

The current MFF's third heading can be separated into two categories: agriculture and maritime policy, and environment and climate action. The heading has an allocation of €400 billion, which makes up about 33 percent of the total EU budget. Most of the money under this heading is allocated to policy preferences. The remainder is allocated to EPGs.

A1.3.1 Agriculture and maritime policy

European Agricultural Guarantee Fund and European Agricultural Fund for Rural Development (EAGF, €291 billion, and EAFRD, €87 billion)

The EU's Common Agricultural Policy (CAP), which accounts for about 31 percent of MFF spending, serves a variety of purposes, which complicates the classification of these goods as either European public goods or others. The CAP has several general and specific objectives, which can be categorised into three clusters of objectives (Regulation (EU) 2021/2115,

Article 5 and 6).

The first relates to food security, with its focus on supporting *"viable farm income and resilience of the agricultural sector"* and fostering a competitive *"agricultural sector ensuring long-term food security"* (Regulation (EU) 2021/2115, Article 6(a)). Food security was defined by the 1996 World Food Summit as physical and economic access to sufficient safe and nutritious food that meets people's dietary needs and food preferences for an active and healthy life[52]. It can be argued that food security is an EPG insofar as it is an essential component of economic and social resilience. The externalities are significant, to the extent that, were food security supplied at national level only, EU members may have an incentive to free ride on the food security provided by other EU members in order to divert their own resources to other spending priorities[53]. However, even with food security as a public good, direct income support, which accounts for most of the spending under the two CAP funds, is not a suitable tool to achieve the objective. Income support – as expressed in the EU Treaties as an objective – is not a public good as such but rather a (social and re-distributional) policy preference. In addition, the evidence suggests that a reduction (or removal) of CAP spending would not impact food security to a harmful degree, indicating that direct income support only serves a limited purpose in promoting food security (JRC, 2017). Removal of all direct income support, in combination with a more open trade policy, would even lead to price reductions, while the EU would still have an aggregate trade surplus in agricultural products. Moreover, Darvas

52 World Bank Group, 'What is Food Security?' undated, https://www.worldbank.org/en/topic/agriculture/brief/food-security-update/what-is-food-security.

53 Free-riding on food security provided by other EU countries might lead to a risk of eventual export controls, and thereby inadequate access to food from other EU countries, in emergency situations. However, Article 36 of the TFEU allows export controls only in exceptional cases, while the European Commission reversed restrictive measures imposed by a few EU members during the COVID-19 pandemic and the Ukraine war.

(2019) demonstrated that food security, measured by the Economist Intelligence Unit's indicator, is slightly worse in the EU than in the United States, Australia, Canada and New Zealand, four countries that provide much less support to agricultural producers than the EU.

The second cluster of CAP objectives seeks to *"support and strengthen environmental protection"*, with a focus on *"contributing to climate change mitigation and adaptation"* and fostering sustainable development (Regulation (EU) 2021/2115, Article 5). Agriculture is a major emitter and polluter and studies show that its climate impact would decrease in the EU if emissions were reduced by the removal of the CAP, with lower emissions mostly driven by a decrease in EU production (JRC, 2017).

The third cluster of objectives aims to *"strengthen the socio-economic fabric of rural areas"* (Regulation (EU) 2021/2115, Article 5(c)). To that end, the CAP seeks to *"facilitate sustainable business development in rural areas"* and to *"attract and sustain young farmers and new farmers and facilitate sustainable business development in rural areas"* (Regulation (EU) 2021/2115, Article 6(g)). It also seeks to further *"local development in rural areas"*. Regional and local imperatives to preserve the character and landscape of rural regions are not genuinely European but rather represent policy preferences. This is because there are no cross-border externalities, and rural areas should be maintained and protected in accordance with national and regional preferences.

A different classification is warranted for some aspects of the European Agricultural Guarantee Fund. Eco-schemes, which focus on supporting farmers in implementing sustainable practices, provide income support the condition of implementation of environmental measures. They support farmers in adopting practices that minimise the negative impacts of agriculture on the environment and climate, and help them evolve towards more sustainable farming models. Insofar as such schemes contribute to environmental protection as a global public good, there is a rationale to qualify them as serving an EPG.

Likewise, the European Maritime, Fisheries and Aquaculture Fund can be likened to the protection of EPGs. The Fund aims at food security, sustainably managed seas and oceans and the growth of a blue economy. With marine resources and fishing resources as classical public goods characterised by negative externalities in the form of national incentives to overfish, the centralised regulation and budgeting of maritime resources can be justified in order to avoid negative externalities.

In conclusion, the current design of the EU's agricultural policy is largely dominated by direct income support, which fails to serve food security as an EPG. Furthermore, income support is not a public good in itself but rather a policy preference.

A1.3.2 Environment and climate action

Programme for Environment and Climate Action (LIFE) (€5 billion)

Climate and environmental protection are classical public goods, and their cross-border effects give them an EPG character. The LIFE programme aims primarily to contribute to the shift towards a sustainable and climate-neutral economy, in order to protect, restore and improve the quality of the environment, including the air, water and soil. LIFE thus undertakes activities with an EPG character.

Just Transition Fund (€8 billion)

The JTF supports the territories most affected by the transition to climate neutrality, in order to prevent regional inequalities from increasing, in line with the aim of EU cohesion policy to reduce regional disparities and to address structural changes. Specifically, the JTF aims to enable *"regions and people to address the social, employment, economic and environmental impacts of the transition towards the Union's 2030 targets for energy and climate"* (Regulation (EU) 2021/1056, Article 2). The JTF thus does not aim primarily at tackling climate change or environmental protection. It is not concerned with climate as an EPG. Rather, it addresses distributive concerns associated with climate change, which will disproportionately affect certain vulnerable groups (regions, workers, SMEs).

Pursuing re-distributive aims does not constitute an EPG. Re-distribution serves to smooth the effect of certain market outcomes or policy measures, but does not exhibit externalities or economies of scale. Rather, policy preferences as to how different groups should benefit from re-distribution are rooted in diverse national preferences. Countries should decide how they want to compensate regions, companies and citizens affected by climate change and how they prioritise between up- and reskilling of workers, investment in SMEs or offering funds to regions to create new firms.

A1.3.3 Heading 3: summary

Figure A3 summarises the previous sections and classifies spending by programme. Large parts of the spending under this heading fall under policy preferences. This is mostly driven by the EAGF and the EAFRD, which constitute direct income support. Only genuine contributions to environmental action are considered to be spending on EPGs.

Figure A3: Categorisation by programme, Heading 3 (%)

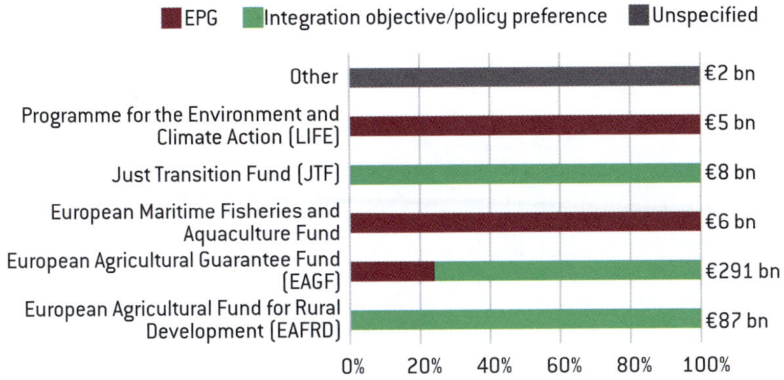

Sources: Bruegel. Note: 'other' includes budget items categorised as other and decentralised agencies.

A1.4 Heading 4: Migration and Border Management (€26 billion)

Programmes under this heading seek to tackle challenges linked to migration and the management of the EU's external borders. The heading has €26 billion allocated to it, or about 2 percent of the EU budget. Most of this heading is allocated to EPGs. The remainder falls under unspecified items, which are minor in the context of the overall EU budget.

Asylum, Migration and Integration Fund and Integrated Border Management Fund (€10 billion and €7 billion)

The EU is largely without internal barriers to the free movement of people. Individuals within the EU can move freely, with EU countries having limited tools to control incoming flows. Consequently, asylum and migration policies create externalities. When countries have different asylum and migration laws and practices, these differences can impact other states. This provides a rationale for centralising the control of migration flows.

Protecting the EU's external border from illegal immigration is an example of a 'weakest-link' public good. It creates externalities because insufficient or ineffective border protection in only one EU country can undermine security for all members.

There is thus a solid case to treat asylum and migration rules and border management as European public goods. The Asylum, Migration and Integration Fund seeks to secure the efficient management of migration flows and the implementation of the common policy on asylum (Regulation (EU) No 516/2014, Article 3). It strengthens the Common European Asylum System, including its external aspects. It is of common interest that the Fund should contribute to effective strategies for return of third-country nationals, and effective readmission to countries of origin and transit. Meanwhile, immigration is an NPG with significant variance (cultural, economic and social) in terms of national migration preferences. This is why the Fund explicitly *"safeguard*[s] *the integrity of the immigration systems of Member States"* (Regulation (EU) 2021/1147).

Similarly, the European Integrated Border Management Fund protects the EU's external borders, implemented by the European Border and Coast Guard as a shared responsibility with the national authorities. Because external borders are a weakest-link public good, it is essential that illegal immigration and cross-border crime are detected and prevented, and that migratory movements are managed effectively.

A1.4.1 Heading 4: summary

Figure A4 summarises the previous section. All programmes under this heading can be classified as EPGs.

Figure A4: Overview of categorisation by programme, Heading 4 (%)

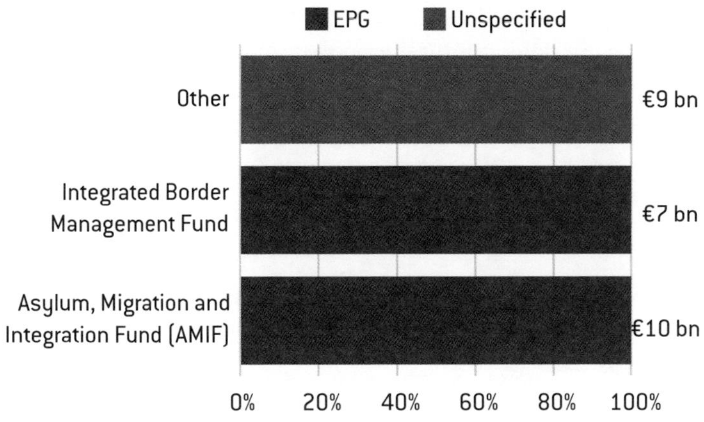

Sources: Bruegel. Note: 'other' includes budget items categorised as other and decentralised agencies.

A1.5 Heading 5: Security and Defence (€14 billion)

This heading includes programmes that have the role of improving the security of European citizens, strengthening Europe's defence capacities and providing the tools needed to respond to internal and external security challenges, which EU countries alone are not able to deal with effectively. The heading has €14 billion allocated, or about 1 percent of the total EU budget. Most of this heading is allocated to EPGs.

Security and the prevention of terrorism, radicalisation and organised crime are public goods with strong European character. The free movement of persons is guaranteed in the EU, but renders all EU members vulnerable to security threats. The threat of terrorism or organised crime can spread easily within the EU. Any measure that counters these threats then implies positive spillover effects that countries acting alone would not sufficiently take into account.

Meanwhile, for defence, there are significant economies of scale in areas such as procurement, armaments, weapon standardisation and deployment (Mueller, 2024; Ostanina, 2024). The Treaties do not fully exploit these potential gains, because they constrain the EU's competence for defence, foreign policy and military matters, with decision-making in these areas subject to unanimity, with *"operations having military or defence implications"* even forbidden (Brøgger, 2024). Unanimity may be justified from a fiscal-federalism perspective when preferences are highly varied. Though opinion surveys show a high degree of public support for EU action (as they do for common defence and security policy)[54], defence remains at the core of state sovereignty.

A1.5.1 Security

Internal Security Fund (€2 billion)

The Internal Security Fund aims to help ensure a high level of security in the EU, in particular by preventing and combating terrorism and radicalisation, serious and organised crime and cybercrime. Protecting the EU from these threats to security implies large positive spillovers, and security activities may produce economies of scale. The specific objectives of the Internal Security Fund are to produce cross-border benefits, notably by facilitating the exchange of information and strengthening

54 European Commission, 'Standard Eurobarometer 101 - Spring 2024', May 2024, https://europa.eu/eurobarometer/surveys/detail/3216.

the capabilities of EU members in relation to preventing and combating crime, terrorism and radicalisation (Regulation (EU) 2021/1149, Article 3(2)). Country-level action alone would not sufficiently account for the positive spillovers for other EU members.

Nuclear decommissioning (€2 billion)

Likewise, funds for nuclear decommissioning (Lithuania) and nuclear safety and decommissioning (including Bulgaria and Slovakia)[55] offer positive spillovers for other EU countries, associated with the security of operation of nuclear plants. These funds are specifically targeted at decommissioning specific Soviet-designed nuclear reactors that are not considered safe in the EU.

A1.5.2 Defence

European Defence Fund (EDF, €8 billion)

The EDF incentivises and supports collaborative, cross-border defence research and development. By adding to national efforts, EDF promotes cooperation between EU companies and research bodies of all sizes and geographic origin. It aims to foster the competitiveness and inventiveness in terms of the defence contribution to the EU's strategic autonomy.

The EDF focuses on funding projects that *"have a clear added value for the Union"* (Regulation (EU) 2021/697, paragraph 37). This underlines both the possibility of taking advantage of economies of scale and positive externalities. The Fund also supports cooperative programmes that would not happen without an EU contribution and, by supporting R&D activities, provides the necessary incentives to boost cooperation at each stage of the industrial cycle.

55 The decommissioning refers specifically to old Soviet-design nuclear reactors that are not considered safe compared to other nuclear reactors. At the times of their accession to the EU, Bulgaria, Slovakia and Lithuania agreed to shut down such power plants.

Military Mobility (€2 billion)

Similar considerations apply to Military Mobility. The Fund concentrates on defence activities of cross-border concern, such as the deployment of military forces in reaction to crises at the EU's external borders. It funds infrastructure where necessary for transnational movement of military transport and to reduce delays when granting national permissions for military transits across borders. Such a measure seeks to minimise negative externalities (from national infrastructure bottlenecks or regulatory incompatibilities).

A1.5.3 Heading 5: summary

Figure A5 plots the classification of Heading 5 programmes. All programmes under this heading can be classified as EPGs.

Figure A5: Overview of categorisation by programme, Heading 5 (%)

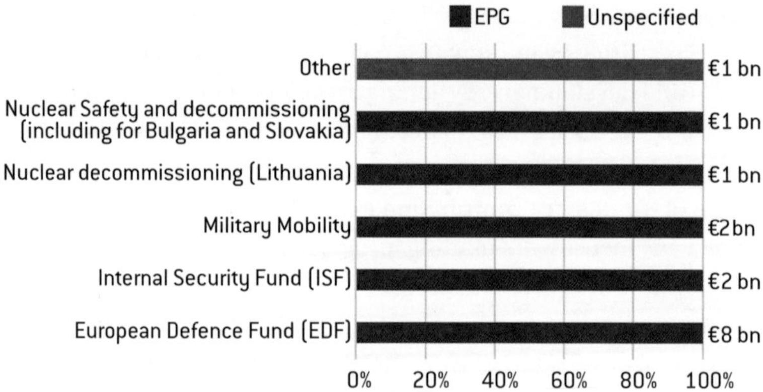

Source: Bruegel. Note: 'other' includes budget items categorised as other and decentralised agencies.

A1.6 Heading 6: Neighbourhood and the World (€110 billion)

Programmes under this heading seek to reinforce the EU's socio-economic impact in its neighbourhood, in developing countries and in the rest of the world. The heading also includes assistance for countries preparing for EU accession. The heading has €110 billion allocated or about 9 percent of the total EU budget (European Commission, 2021c). This heading is fully allocated to EPGs.

A1.6.1 General considerations on external relations as a public good

Neighbourhood policy encompasses the EU's external relations in a wide sense. In general, foreign policy can be a source of externalities and can offer economies of scale, but is often associated with preferences rooted in each country's history, politics and culture.

Negative externalities may arise when the national foreign policies of EU members are inconsistent or even contradictory. The national pursuit of foreign policies is often driven by domestic policy preferences, not taking into account the interests of other countries. In the EU context, purely national foreign policies thus risk adverse effects for other EU countries' national interests.

Closely connected to concerns about externalities, there are also significant economy-of-scale arguments in favour of a Europeanised foreign and security policy. They build on the insight that size and weight in international relations matters – larger countries and coordinated action carry more weight compared to individual members acting individually on the global stage. 'Speaking with one voice' gives each EU country more political and economic weight than speaking with different voices. This applies in particular in times of geopolitical polarisation.

However, foreign policy is considered a national prerogative (GFCC, 2009). Significant differences between the foreign policy preferences of EU countries make a complete surrender of foreign policies from national to EU level unlikely. A mix of centralised policies and decentralised policies seem suitable for untapping economies of scale while also accounting for national preferences.

The EU Treaties include a strong unanimity requirement in the area of Common Foreign and Security Policy (CFSP), meaning EU members control this policy area. The EU has more authority over the conduct of development policy, aimed at sustainable economic, social and environmental development in developing countries, with the primary aim of eradicating poverty (Article 21 (2) TEU). In this area, the EU can adopt policies by qualified majority (Article 208, 209 TFEU).

The objectives underpinning the EU's policies under Heading 6 are to address issues of global concerns and pursue values shared across the EU. Heading 6 policies respond to increased migration and refugee flows, security threats and wider changes in the international and regional contexts (EPRS, 2021). These threats are of equal concern for all EU countries as they are all affected by them because of free movement across the EU. These global concerns are addressed under the heading associated with climate change, security, and migration – concerns that are often considered as global public goods (Barrett, 2007). They are also directly linked to the United Nation's 2030 Sustainable Development Agenda and the implementation of the Paris Climate Agreement.

The intuitive added value of EU action in addressing global public goods is linked to the above considerations on externalities and economies of scale. Harmonised policies leverage the EU's capacities to contribute effectively to sustaining global public goods such as a stable climate, security, poverty reduction and peace. EU neighbourhood policies take advantage of the EU's political and economic clout and the geographic range of its external cooperation, which a single EU country would not be able to achieve.

At the same time, neighbourhood policy contains policies (see below) linked to the CFSP, which concerns more sensitive issues of foreign relations from a sovereignty perspective. It should therefore be emphasised that EU countries retain certain competences in pursuing foreign and neighbourhood policies to account for specific national preferences. The scope of external relations extends beyond the policies undertaken within the MFF (which can be considered EPGs), with other aspects of external relations falling under the category of national public goods.

A1.6.2 External action

Neighbourhood Development and International Cooperation Instrument (NDICI, €71 billion)

The goal of NDICI is to support global public goods including sustainable development, peace and stability, building on the European consensus on development and the UN's 2030 Agenda. It also factors in cross-cutting priorities, such as environmental protection and climate action, and it sets spending targets in line with the SDGs. NDICI has a three-pillar structure:

- Geographical: under this pillar, the aim is to foster cooperation conducive to sustainable economic growth and employment, security and peace. Protecting the rule of law, human rights, the environment and climate action are often viewed as global public goods. Given this global public good character, they should be coordinated at the highest governance level possible, which in our context means the EU level.
- Thematic: this pillar addresses issues linked to the pursuit at global level of the SDGs, including democracy, human rights, civil society, stability and peace, and global challenges.
- Rapid response: this pillar contributes to stability and conflict prevention in situations of urgency, and links humanitarian aid to development action.

Each pillar contains a European element. Since EU countries have a common interest in pursuing objectives of global concern, there is no issue of preference heterogeneity as a counterargument to the economies of scale that EU action entails. We thus consider spending under this instrument as spending on EPGs.

Humanitarian aid (€10 billion)

Humanitarian aid may be subject to slightly different considerations from the public-good perspective. Humanitarian aid may be determined by the preferences of EU members. EU members may prioritise needs differently when providing humanitarian aid, with geographical priorities reflecting the traditional links of EU countries to certain regions (eg former colonies). Humanitarian aid will thus remain, to some extent, an NPG in order to account for these diverse preferences.

However, EU-led humanitarian aid should also focus on major areas of common concern. EU humanitarian aid primarily addresses humanitarian crises resulting from conflicts, global refugee flows or natural disasters linked to climate change. They respond to events of joint European (or even global) concern and may be disconnected from the traditional ties EU countries have with certain regions. Administrative efficiency may add to scale arguments because EU humanitarian aid is deployed in partnership with global bodies such as UN agencies, NGOs and international organisations. Overall, humanitarian aid pursued under Heading 6 serves the delivery of EPGs, while EU countries retain humanitarian aid competence (as a field of shared competence under the Treaty), in that they deliver NPGs from their national budgets.

Common foreign and security policy (CFSP, €2 billion)

CFSP remains a policy field with both European and national public-good elements. While externalities and economies of scale offer strong rationales for centralising CFSP, national prerogatives are associated with foreign policy as an issue of sovereignty. The Treaties therefore give the EU only limited scope for action in this area, and require unanimity. Like humanitarian aid, foreign policy is thus both an EPG and an NPG. Expenditure under Heading 6 leverages those instances where EU centralised action can generate economies of scale through 'speaking with one voice'. In other words, the added value of this expenditure is found in the fact that it makes possible the EU's role as a global player on behalf of and alongside its members (EPRS, 2021). In addition, institutional economies of scale can be realised through the institution of the High Representative of the Union for Foreign Affairs and Security

Policy/Vice-President of the European Commission (HR/VP) and the European External Action Service. These institutions do not replace national diplomatic services, but integrate EU countries' interests when it makes sense to centralise power. In terms of CFSP objectives, the policy pursues issues of global concern by addressing conflict, instability and security threats. We thus categorise spending under this heading as spending on EPGs.

Overseas countries and territories, including Greenland (€444 million)

Cooperation with overseas countries and territories[56] follows a similar logic to NDICI. While not covering the immediate neighbourhood, the policy promotes the EU's special relationship, and its interest in promoting the economic and social development of, those countries and territories and strengthening their ties with the EU. This sub-heading involves competences under the Treaties that are different from NDICI. Like NDICI, this instrument has an EPG character, given the joint interest of EU members in promoting and stabilising the relationships with these territories and regions. This cooperation does not interfere with special national ties, such as that between Denmark and Greenland, which are handled at national level, leaving scope to treat these relationships as NPGs.

A1.6.3 Pre-Accession Assistance

Instrument for Pre-Accession Assistance (€13 billion)

EU countries have a common interest in preparing new members for their accessions. Policies and instruments, such as pre-accession assistance, aim to pave the way for new members to accede to the EU. A centralised approach to this rather than decentralised assistance from current members appears straightforward, with the EU as the coordinator

56 The EU's overseas countries and territories are not sovereign countries but depend to varying degrees on three EU countries, Denmark, France, and the Netherlands, with which they maintain special links. There are 13 such countries and territories.

setting priorities that define administrative, social and economic reforms. By bringing new member states into alignment with the *acquis communautaire* to which all EU members are subject, there is a rationale for centralised action.

A1.6.4 Heading 6: summary

In conclusion, neighbourhoods generally involve both EPGs and NPGs. For this reason, EU members have retained significant foreign policy power, while delegating part of development policy to the EU. Heading 6 expenditure can be considered as financing the European share of the public good, while countries continue to pursue their policies separately. All programmes under this heading can be classified as spending on EPGs (Figure A6).

Figure A6: Overview of categorisation by programme, Heading 6 (%)

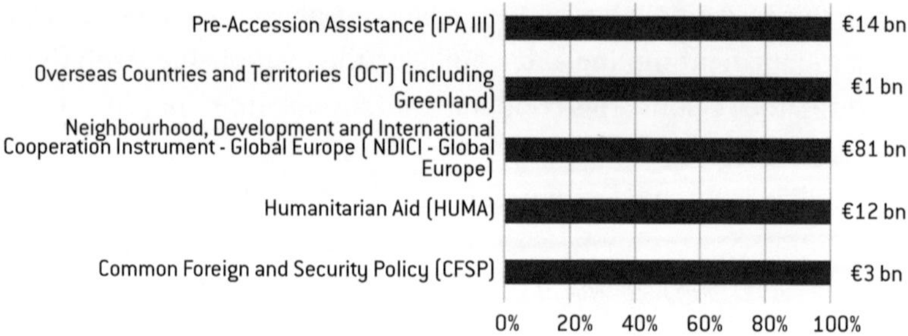

Sources: Bruegel.

Some of these instruments have substantial EPG components. Neighbourhood development, pre-accession assistance and cooperation with overseas territories can be considered as areas for which economies of scale are significant and the preferences of EU members are largely similar. For CFSP, humanitarian aid and the European Facility, strong economies of scale provide a reason to consider these fields as EPGs, but they relate to sensitive issues of state sovereignty with historically and culturally determined military and defence preferences, or, in the case of humanitarian aid, sometimes strong national political and historical ties. It can nevertheless be justified to treat EU spending in these areas as relating to the European interest, while EU members should – and under the EU Treaties can – continue to pursue national policies.

A1.7 Heading 7: European Public Administration (€83 billion)

The European public administration implements policies and programmes in the common EU interest. The public good character of the related spending must be assessed with regard to the human resource budget line. Civil service is non-exclusive to the extent that all citizens have access to the service under non-discrimination rules. Public services can be made divisible and excludable, for instance, by introducing service charges, giving access only to those who pay or individualising charges for collective provision such as rubbish collection (Spicker, 2024). This, however, is not the case with EU public administration.

There is also a broad debate on the extent to which the public sector should be governed by market principles. For our purposes, we can say that public service is instrumental in delivering the public good to citizens. The fundamentals of a functioning state are generally seen as public goods – government services demonstrate that public goods can be human-made (such as public health or defence), and it is public service personnel who perform basic state functions such as the exercise of executive, legislative and judicial powers.

In the EU context judges and administrators at the EU Court of Justice (CJEU) provide legal security and a court system, often seen as a public good (Paine, 2018). Since the CJEU ensures respect for EU laws even when some laws seem contrary to national interest, the CJEU is clearly an EPG. European Parliament members and staff perform the public function of the legislator for the EU as a whole, not following specific national interests. European Commission personnel deliver the functions of the executive. Thus, each of the Heading 7 staff categories can be allocated to a specific state function. The use of the services of these European institutions is non-rival and non-excludable, their operations involve major cross-border externalities by ensuring harmonised application of EU laws and regulations, and there are also scale effects, since centralised safeguarding of the EU Treaties is more effective than if EU countries were to do this under a coordination mechanism. Thus, EU public administration services are EPGs (Figure A7).

The heading has around €83 billion allocated to it, or about 7 percent of the budget.

Figure A7: Overview of categorisation by programme, Heading 7 (%)

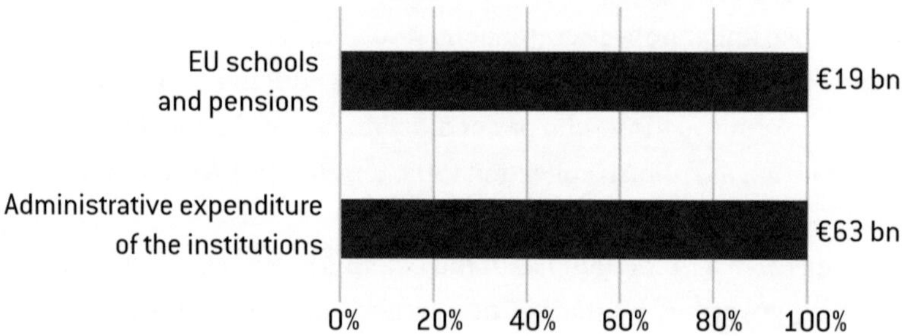

Source: Bruegel.

Annex 2: Overview of EU spending outside the MFF

Assessing the EPG character of some instruments outside the MFF

REACT EU (€51 billion)

REACT-EU was established to address the economic fallout of the COVID-19 pandemic. The programme can provide support for crisis response and crisis repair measures and is intended a bridge to long-term recovery. COVID-19 required a joint response to alleviate its immediate macroeconomic impact. Concentrating aid on particularly vulnerable regions makes sense from a macroeconomic perspective to ensure economic recovery. This EU-wide macroeconomic dimension is further strengthened by the allocation methodology for this funding, which takes full account of the economic and social impact of the crisis on the EU countries, irrespective of regional quotas. With this pandemic focus and the macroeconomic function of REACT-EU, it furthers the EPG of macroeconomic stability.

Recovery and Resilience Facility (€724 billion, €338 billion in grants and €386 billion in loans)

NextGenerationEU was established as a macroeconomic response aimed at securing recovery from COVID-19. In interconnected economies like those of the EU – with most countries sharing the same currency – macroeconomic stability is no longer solely a national concern. This is especially true when a symmetric shock affects the entire EU.

EU members with low levels of public debt have the fiscal space to support themselves, whereas highly indebted countries face fiscal constraints. While a moral hazard problem exists, with some countries potentially pursuing irresponsible fiscal policies in good times, expecting low-debt countries to assist them during downturns, economic resilience is a public good (Buti and Papaconstantinou, 2022). After the devastating human and economic impact of COVID-19, saving lives and fostering economic recovery became common goals.

By granting the EU an exceptional capacity for debt financing, the union leveraged economies of scale, utilising the combined solvency of all 27 EU members – an opportunity that would have remained unrealised with purely national fiscal responses. As a result, both the centralised funding and the allocation of resources have contributed to serving European public goods.

With macroeconomic stability as the primary EPG supplied through the Recovery and Resilience Facility (RRF – the main component of NGEU), the design of the allocation scheme further strengthens other EPGs. The focus on climate-oriented expenditures as fixed quota within the expenditure allocation enhances resilience and furthers the protection of the climate.

European Peace Facility (EPF, €17 billion)

The European Peace Facility was created outside the MFF as a mechanism to fund common foreign and security policy operations with military and defence implications. Placing it outside the MFF avoids the restrictions under the EU Treaties on financing operational expenditure with military/defence implications (Article 41(2) TEU). With Russia's war against Ukraine, the purpose and public good character of the Facility came to the fore. Irrespective of the legal treatment of defence-related expenditure, the threat to peace is a concern for all European countries. Deferring the defence of Ukraine to individual countries only is implausible. Security is a European public good and military threats affect all EU members.

At the same time, the Treaty restrictions indicate a variance in political preferences, by protecting neutral states that insisted on the Treaty ban on financing military operations. These countries have treated defence as purely an NPG. Because EU countries finance the

Peace Facility off budget, national prerogatives are respected. The EPF thus has the character of a 'club public good' insofar as not all EU members are obliged to support the funding and different national preferences in the core national concern of defence are respected.

Table A1: Overview of EU funds outside the MFF

Fund / Instrument	Purpose	Funding source	Managing body	Period	Amount
		Funds related to the green transition			
Innovation Fund	Support low-carbon innovation & energy transition	EU ETS revenues	European Commission	Temporary, 2021-2030	€4 billion annual (carbon price of €75/tCO2) , €40 billion over period
Modernisation Fund	Energy transition in lower-income EU states	EU ETS revenues	Member States and EIB	Temporary, 2021-2030	€5.7 billion annual, (carbon price of €75/tCO2) , €57 billion over period
Social Climate Fund	Support low-income households for climate transitions	EU ETS 2 revenues (75%) and MS co-financing (25%)	European Commission / Member States	Temporary, 2026-2032	€12.4 billion annual, €86.7 billion over period
Just Transition Mechanism – Pillar 3	Loans to public sector for transition projects	Partial MFF funding + EIB loans	European Commission & EIB	Temporary, 2021–2027	Loans: €6-8 billion, grants: €1.3 billion over period
		Funds related to defence and security			
European Peace Facility (EPF)	Fund military/ defence support to partners	Off-budget (direct MS contributions)	European External Action Service (EEAS)	Temporary, 2021–2027	€2.4 billion annual, €17 billion over period

Ukraine Facility	Flagship support programme for Ukraine	Partial MFF funding (grants) + borrowing on capital markets (EU bonds) backed by headroom (loans)	European Commission	Temporary, 2024-2027	up to €50 billion (mix of loans and grants)
Funds related to emergency relief (for economic and financial stability)					
European Stability Mechanism (ESM) (former EFSF)	Financial aid to euro area countries	Intergovernmental capital & markets	Intergovernmental (Eurogroup)	Permanent, established in 2012	paid-in capital (€71 billion) and callable capital (€709 billion)
└─**European Financial Stabilisation Mechanism (EFSM)**	Crisis loans to EU countries (legacy)	EU-guaranteed borrowing backed by headroom	European Commission	Permanent, established in 2010 (legacy item that remains active)	*Ad hoc*
Single Resolution Fund (SRF)	Bank resolution in the euro area	Banking sector levies	Single Resolution Board (SRB)	Permanent, established in 2016 (operational start)	1% of covered deposits of Banking Union banks (around €75 billion in 2023)
MacroFinancial Assistance+ (MFA+) / MFA to Ukraine	Special MFA instrument to Ukraine	Borrowing on capital markets (EU bonds) backed by headroom and guarantees by Member States	European Commission	Special instrumentson top of standard MFA	€18 billion in 2023 (MFA+, repayment beginning 2033)

Balance of Payments (BoP) Facility	Assistance to countries with difficulties re: BoP	Borrowing on capital markets (EU bonds) backed by headroom	European Commission and international institutions (e.g. IMF)	Permanent, established in 2002	*Ad hoc*
Support to mitigate Unemployment Risks in an Emergency (SURE)	temporary support to fund job-saving initiatives	Borrowing on capital markets (EU bonds), backed by headroom + €25 billion in direct irrevocable callable guarantees from EU countries	European Commission	Temporary, 2020-2022	Up to €100 billion in loans (actual funding raised: €98.4 Billion), about €32.8 Billion annually
NextGenerationEU (NGEU)	Temporary recovery instrument (post-COVID)	Borrowing on capital markets (EU bonds), backed by headroom	European Commission	Temporary, 2021–2026	€135 billion annually, or €806.9 Billion in total (or €750 billion in 2018 prices)
└─ **Recovery and Resilience Facility**	Core of NGEU, reforms & investments for recovery	NGEU	European Commission	Temporary, 2021–2026	Planned: €121 billion annually, or €723.8 billion in total (loans and grants) Allocated: €93 billion annually, or €648 billion in total (grants and loans), where €357 billion in grants (out of which €338 billion through borrowing, €17.3 billion through ETS revenue and €1.6 billion from the Brexit Adjustment Reserve) and €291 billion in loans called

└ **RescEU**	Civil protection reserve (e.g. masks, medical transport)	NGEU, top-up for budget item Union Civil Protection Mechanism	European Commission	Temporary, 2021–2023	€0.7 billion annually, or €2 billion in total (loans and grants)
└ **REACT-EU**	Immediate COVID-19 recovery via Cohesion Funds	NGEU	Member States via Cohesion rules	Temporary, 2021–2023	€34 billion annually, or €51 billion in total (loans and grants)
Other funds					
Euratom loans to MS	Finance back-to-back loans to investment projects related to nuclear power generation and the nuclear fuel cycle	Borrowing on capital markets (EU bonds) backed by headroom	European Commission	Permanent, established 1977	Maximum of €4 billion outstanding back-to-back loans, *ad hoc*
Flexibility instruments associated with the EU budget maximum additional amount that can be used for special instruments in 2021–2027 will be around EUR 21 billion					
Flexibility Instrument	Finance actions that cannot get funding via other sources of the budget	Flexibility under MFF	European Commission	2021-2027 (MFF)	Annual allocation of € 0.92 Billion (in 2018 prices)
Single Margin instrument	Funding not used as planned can be redirected to where it is needed the most	Flexibility under MFF	European Commission	2021-2027 (MFF)	Funding not used as planned

European Globalisation Adjustment Fund	Help reintegrate workers who have lost their jobs due to globalisation into the labour market	Flexibility under MFF	European Commission	2021-2027 (MFF)	Maximum annual amount of € 0.19 Billion (in 2018 prices)
Solidarity and Emergency Aid Reserve	Help tackle emergency situations (e.G. Natural disasters or public health crises)	Flexibility under MFF	European Commission	2021-2027 (MFF)	Maximum annual amount of € 1.2 Billion (in 2018 prices)
Brexit Adjustment Reserve	Reserve is aimed at countering the adverse consequences of the departure of the United Kingdom from the EU in the worst-affected Member States and sectors	Flexibility under MFF	European Commission	2021-2027 (MFF)	Overall size of € 5 billion (in 2018 prices)